Workshop on Language Processing and Crisis Information 2013

Held at the 6th International Joint Conference on Natural Language Processing (IJCNLP 2013)

Nagoya, Japan
14-18 October 2013

ISBN: 978-1-62993-545-4

Printed from e-media with permission by:

Curran Associates, Inc.
57 Morehouse Lane
Red Hook, NY 12571

CURRAN ASSOCIATES INC. proceedings.com

Some format issues inherent in the e-media version may also appear in this print version.

Printed by Curran Associates, Inc. (2014)

For permission requests, please contact the Association for Computational Linguistics at the address below.

Association for Computational Linguistics
209 N. Eighth Street
Stroudsburg, Pennsylvania 18360

Phone: 1-570-476-8006
Fax: 1-570-476-0860

acl@aclweb.org

Additional copies of this publication are available from:

Curran Associates, Inc.
57 Morehouse Lane
Red Hook, NY 12571 USA
Phone: 845-758-0400
Fax: 845-758-2634
Email: curran@proceedings.com
Web: www.proceedings.com

We wish to thank our sponsors and supporters!

Platinum Sponsors

NLP

www.anlp.jp

Silver Sponsors

Google™

www.google.com

Bronze Sponsors

Rakuten

www.rakuten.com

Supporters

NAGOYA CONVENTION
& VISITORS BUREAU

Nagoya Convention & Visitors Bureau

We wish to thank our organizers!

Organizers

Asian Federation of Natural Language Processing (AFNLP)

Toyohashi University of Technology

Introduction

The past few years have seen a number of horrible, high-profile crises, including the Earthquake and Massive Tsunami in Eastern Japan, and Hurricane Sandy, which caused billions of dollars of damage across the Caribbean and east coast of the United States. Given the importance and urgency of response to these disasters, there has been a heightening interest in crisis informatics, or the use of information technology to improve the speed and effectiveness of disaster response.

One particular area where information technology holds particular promise is in the processing of language. For example, in times of crisis, valuable information about the current state of events in disaster-affected areas is broadcast by various individuals or organizations, in disparate locations, and in varying forms, the majority of which involve some sort of natural language. In situations such as these, it is extremely important to be able to aggregate and filter every bit of available information, and deliver it as quickly and accurately as possible to those who could benefit by its provision.

In this workshop, we hope to provide a venue to propose new techniques for processing language related to times of crisis. In particular, we place a focus on the role that language and language processing technology can play in crisis response, analysis of social dynamics in times of crisis, and increasing preparedness for crises that may occur in the future.

Organizers:

Kentaro Inui (Tohoku University, Japan)
Hideto Kazawa (Google Japan)
Graham Neubig (NAIST, Japan)
Masao Utiyama (NICT, Japan)

Program Committee/Reviewers:

Eiji Aramaki (Kyoto University, Japan)
Kevin Duh (NAIST, Japan)
Atsushi Fujita (Future University Hakodate, Japan)
Masato Hagiwara (Rakuten Institute of Technology, USA)
Mai Miyabe (University of Tokyo, Japan)
Robert Munro (Idibon, USA)
Koji Murakami (Rakuten Institute of Technology, USA)
Kiyonori Ohtake (NICT, Japan)
Kate Starbird (University of Washington, USA)
Irina Temnikova (Bulgarian Academy of Sciences, Bulgaria)
Kentaro Torisawa (NICT, Japan)

Table of Contents

Workshop Program

Monday October 14, 2013

(11:00) Session 1

An Evidence Based Earthquake Detector using Twitter
Bella Robinson, Robert Power and Mark Cameron

Computer-assisted Structuring of Emergency Management Information: A Project Note
Yotaro Watanabe, Kentaro Inui, Shingo Suzuki, Hiroko Koumoto, Mitsuhiro Higashida, Yuji Maeda and Katsumi Iwatsuki

(13:30) Session 2

Rescue Activity for the Great East Japan Earthquake Based on a Website that Extracts Rescue Requests from the Net
Shin Aida, Yasutaka Shindo and Masao Utiyama

A Framework and Tool for Collaborative Extraction of Reliable Information
Graham Neubig, Shinsuke Mori and Masahiro Mizukami

Extracting and Aggregating False Information from Microblogs
Naoaki Okazaki, Keita Nabeshima, Kento Watanabe, Junta Mizuno and Kentaro Inui

Returning-Home Analysis in Tokyo Metropolitan Area at the time of the Great East Japan Earthquake using Twitter Data
Yusuke Hara

BahaBa: A Route Generator System for Mobile Devices
Ralph Vincent Regalado, Michael Benedict Haw, Matthew Alexis Martinez, Lowie Santiaguel and Patrick Lawrence Tamayo

An Evidence Based Earthquake Detector using Twitter

Bella Robinson
bella.robinson@csiro.au

Robert Power
robert.power@csiro.au

Mark Cameron
mark.cameron@csiro.au

CSIRO Computational Informatics
G.P.O. Box 664
Canberra, ACT 2601, Australia

Abstract

This paper presents a notification system to identify earthquakes from first-hand reports published on Twitter. Tweets from target regions in Australia and New Zealand are checked for earthquake keyword frequency bursts and then processed to identify evidence of an earthquake.

The benefit of our earthquake detector is that it relies on evidence of firsthand 'felt' reports from Twitter, provides an indication of the earthquake intensity and will be the trigger for further classification of Tweets for impact analysis.

We describe how the detector has been incrementally improved, most notably by the introduction of a text classifier. During its initial five months of operation the system has generated 49 notifications of which 29 related to real earthquake events.

1 Introduction

Australia and New Zealand have experienced a number of large scale disaster events in recent years. Christchurch New Zealand suffered two earthquakes of magnitude 7.1 (4 September 2010) and 6.3 (22 February 2011) with significant aftershocks continuing around this time. While there were no reported fatalities for the first event, there were 185 deaths in the second with widespread damage and an estimated NZ$15 billion in reconstruction costs (Bruns and Burgess, 2012).

In Australia, the Victorian 2009 Black Saturday Bushfires killed 173 people, impacted 78 towns with loses estimated at A$2.9 billion (Stephenson et al., 2012). The 2010-2011 floods in Queensland affected 70 towns, including the state capital Brisbane, and caused infrastructure damage of A$8 billion (RBA, 2011). Tropical cyclone Yasi (Feb 2011) was a category 5 system that crossed northern Queensland causing an estimated A$800 million in damage (Qld Budget, 2011).

In order to effectively prepare and respond to emergency situations it is critical that emergency managers and crisis coordinators have relevant and reliable information. In Australia, this knowledge is traditionally obtained from official authoritative sources such as the state emergency services and first responder agencies, such as the police force, fire and rescue and rural fire services. Traditional news media (television, news agency web sites and sometimes radio) is also used to provide intelligence about events.

Social media has been recognised as a potential new source of information for emergency managers (Anderson, 2012; Bruns et al., 2012; Alliance Strategic Research, 2011; Lindsay, 2011; Charlton, 2012). However, it is mostly used 'passively' in that during crisis events the emergency services agencies use social media to disseminate information to the community and receive user feedback on their advice (Lindsay, 2011). In order for the full potential of social media to be realised, it needs to be embraced as a new 'channel' of information where the evolving situational awareness of events can be improved.

This paper presents a case study outlining the use of Twitter to detect earthquakes. The detector generates email notifications summarising the Tweets contributing to the alert and includes an indication of the intensity of the event.

2 Background

2.1 Earthquake Detection

An earthquake results from movement in the Earth's crust and different scales have been defined to measure them. The moment magnitude and Richter scales measure the energy released whereas the Modified Mercalli Intensity (MMI) scale (Eiby, 1966) measures the effects.

An earthquake in the ocean may produce a tsunami. The tsunamis in Indonesia and Thailand on 26 December 2004 occurred with little warning to the communities affected. The Japan tsunami of 11 March 2011 was preceded by warnings however its size was greater than anticipated and resulted in widespread damage and loss of life.

Tsunami warning centres exist world wide. They rely on the identification of earthquakes and information from networks of sea level monitoring equipment, such as coastal tide gauges and deep ocean tsunami sensors, in conjunction with software models to determine the existence of tsunamis, their intensity and trajectory.

Identifying earthquakes is a time consuming and complex task performed by highly trained seismologists. Verification of an earthquake event requires the use of a global network of seismic stations to determine the precise location and magnitude of the earthquake. This process can take up to 15 minutes from when the earthquake occurred.

While some countries and regions have a highly sophisticated and dense network of seismic sensors, for example Japan[1] has over 4000 sensors and the state of California[2] in the USA has over 3000 sensors, other countries including some that are highly earthquake prone do not. Australia[3] which is roughly 20 times the area of Japan has only 70 sensors, earthquake prone Indonesia[4] is roughly 5 times the size of Japan and has only 400 sensors and New Zealand[5] which is roughly one third smaller than Japan and also earthquake prone has only 300 sensors.

Recent studies (Sakaki et al., 2010; Earle et al., 2012; Sakaki et al., 2013; Robinson et al., 2013) indicate that when an earthquake event occurs in populated regions, reports on Twitter can provide a faster method of detection compared to traditional approaches. The role of seismologists to verify and scientifically characterise earthquakes can be augmented by crowd sourced information that provides both an early warning and evidence of the impact experienced by the community affected.

[1] http://www.jma.go.jp/jma/en/Activities/earthquake.html

[2] http://www.cisn.org/instr/

[3] http://www.ga.gov.au/earthquakes/seismicSearch.do

[4] http://aeic.bmg.go.id/aeic/indonesia.html

[5] http://info.geonet.org.nz/display/equip/Equipment

It is important to note that an earthquake's magnitude and location cannot reliably be used to infer the impact on a community. For example, the first Christchurch earthquake mentioned above caused damage to buildings, but fortunately there was no loss of life. The one that followed was smaller and technically an aftershock of the previous one (Bruns and Burgess, 2012), but resulted in fatalities and extensive damage.

2.2 Related Work

Studies of Twitter communications during crises and natural disasters such as earthquakes, have found strong temporal correlations with real-world events (Mendoza et al., 2010). Applying NLP classifiers to extracting situation awareness information has been investigated by Verma et al. (2011). Again that study finds there is strong correlation between data collected in a localised region about a local event and evidence of situation awareness Tweet content.

Several systems have been developed for the automatic detection of earthquakes via Twitter. Earle et al. (2012) describe a detection system operating over a filtered Tweet stream. Importantly, Tweets are filtered if they contain http, RT or @ symbols or more than n tokens. Their detection algorithm is based on a modified short-term long-term ratio over this filtered stream. The filters and n token heuristic aim to account for non first-hand reports. Sakaki et al. (2010) and Sakaki et al. (2013) have deployed a functional system in Japan that uses natural language processing techniques to classify Tweets containing specific keywords, such as *earthquake* or *shaking*. Positively classified Tweets are then used to generate a probabilistic spatio-temporal model of the event and particle filtering is used to estimate the earthquake location. Users of both systems are notified of a potential earthquake via email.

2.3 Social Media Platform

In order to demonstrate the benefit of information published on social media for emergency management we have been continuously collecting Tweets originating from Australia and New Zealand since March 2010 (Cameron et al., 2012). To date, over one billion Tweets have been processed at approximately 1500 per minute. These Tweets have been used to: experiment with alternative algorithms for event detection; develop clustering techniques for condensing and summarising information content; develop language models to characterise the expected discourse on Twitter; develop an alerting system based on the language model to detect deviations from the expected discourse; train and evaluate text classification systems; and perform forensic analysis.

The aim is to develop a near-real-time platform that monitors Twitter to identify events and improve the situational awareness of emergency events for emergency managers and crisis coordinators. While originally developed for Australia and New Zealand, the technology can be configured and deployed for any region. Additional work would be required to process languages that do not use spaces to separated words.

3 The Problem

The task is to quickly and reliably detect, locate and estimate the intensity of earthquakes as reported on Twitter. Earthquake detection provides a targeted use case to test our social media platform. While early detection of earthquakes can currently be achieved using traditional methods, for example using seismic equipment, this process is tuned to accurately locate and measure the *magnitude* of an earthquake: the energy released. An important distinction is the earthquake *intensity*: the effect of the earthquake to people and the impact on the natural and built environments.

People Tweeting in response to an earthquake event effectively become sensors indicating the scale of the event in terms of the number of Tweets collected. The Tweet content can also be analysed to provide an indication of impact severity. These measures, the scale in terms of number of Tweets and the severity in terms of Tweet content, can be combined to provide an earthquake intensity measure analogous to the MMI scale.

3.1 Preliminary Work

The Social Media platform described in Section 2.3 was configured using heuristics to identify firsthand 'felt' reports as evidence of earthquake events. The heuristics were arrived at after examining the Tweets for all historical earthquake related alerts reported by the system.

The alerts are generated in reference to a background language model. In essence, a five minute buffer of the most recent Tweets is maintained where the frequency of words in the buffer is compared against an historical model of expected word frequencies. When the observed word frequency deviates significantly from the historical model, an alert is generated. The buffer is advanced in one minute increments thus producing a new set of alerts each minute. These alerts are recorded by the platform in a database.

Note that the alerts generated by this method correspond to bursts of unusual word frequencies with respect to the historical language model, not to bursts in the arrival rate of Tweets.

To determine the heuristics to use, 12 months of historical earthquake alerts were analysed. In summary, the process involves filtering alerts generated from the social media platform that match earthquake related keywords, testing the currency of the alert (only consider the first alert generated and not subsequent ones), determining if the Tweets producing the alert are close geographically and measuring the retweet ratio (since a retweet cannot be a firsthand 'felt' report).

3.2 The Heuristic Detector

An earthquake detector was developed as described above. Heuristic thresholds were identified in reference to the earthquake events recorded in the 12 month analysis period. When an earthquake event is found an email notification is generated summarising the Tweet information and heuristic results.

This email is sent to the Joint Australian Tsunami Warning Centre (JATWC) who have responsibility to detect earthquakes in the oceans around Australia, to identify potential tsunami events when such earthquakes are identified and to issue tsunami warnings as required.

This detector has been in operation since mid December 2012. During the first five months of operation, 49 earthquake emails were generated. These notifications were manually reviewed and 29 found to correspond with real earthquake events (*true positives (TP)*). The remaining 20 (*false positives (FP)*) were a result of discussions about earthquakes but not prompted by an event.

A review after two months of operation identified changes to the thresholds used for the heuristics. Doing so improved the results, greatly reducing the *false positives*, but required extensive work to investigate the detected events by cross referencing with seismically verified earthquakes as listed by New Zealand's GeoNet[5] and Geoscience Australia (GA)[3].

4 Introducing a Classifier

The task of detecting earthquakes from Twitter was then considered as a text classification problem. The results obtained in the first five months of operation described above provided a set of earthquake related Tweets that could be labelled as a test set. These Tweets were used to train a classifier configured using a comprehensive range of features. This process forms the basis of our paper: improving the accuracy of the earthquake detector by incorporating the use of a text classifier to predict whether individual Tweets are instances of firsthand earthquake reports.

The following sections describe the journey we have taken in developing a classifier for earthquake detection.

4.1 Earthquake Alert Annotations

The process of reviewing the performance of the heuristic detector involved examination of the Tweets contributing to each earthquake related alert and labelling them as evidence of firsthand earthquake reports. This produced a collection of 237 alerts, of which 45 contained examples of firsthand earthquake reports. Reviewing the existing heuristic detector's performance in terms of these alerts we achieve an F1 score of 0.667 (TP=23,FP=11,TN=181,FN=12).

Figure 1 shows the number of Tweets that include the word 'earthquake' and contribute to an earthquake alert. These numbers are aggregates of multiple alerts for time periods from mid December 2012. There are 34 such time periods with a total of over 8000 Tweets. 15 of these time periods have 50 or less Tweets in them, 14 have more than 100 and two have more than one thousand.

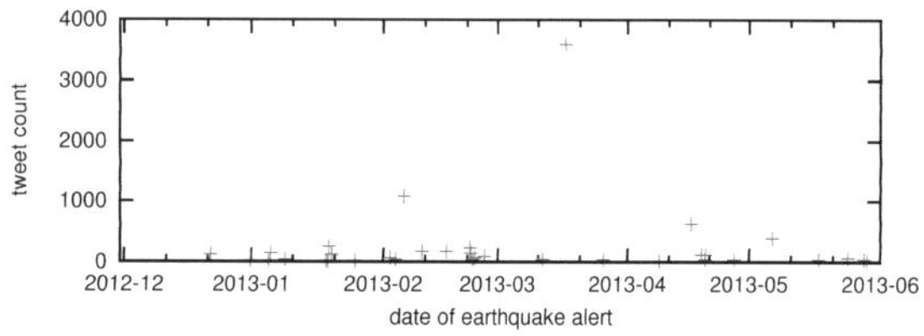

Figure 1: 'earthquake' alerts

The same data is plotted in Figure 2 showing more detail for the time periods with fewer Tweets.

4.2 Initial Training Data

Training data was needed to configure the classifier. Initially, sets of suggested positive and negative Tweets were generated by using the alert

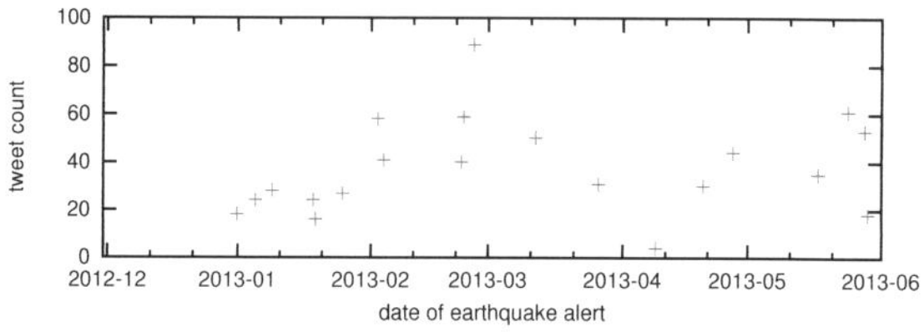

Figure 2: 'earthquake' alerts: zoomed

data identified in the alert annotation step outlined above. All Tweets contributing to an alert labelled as positive were initially labelled as positive and the reverse for the negative alerts. To increase the sample size, Tweets were also gathered from follow-up alerts that occurred within five minutes of the initial alert.

It is important to note that retweets have been excluded from the classification process: by definition a retweet cannot be a firsthand report of feeling an earthquake.

The suggested positive and negative Tweets were then examined individually to adjust the labels when incorrect. The results of this initial Tweet annotation phase produced a set of 1604 labelled Tweets, with 868 being positive and 736 negative. Examples are shown in Table 1.

4.3 Feature Selection

As noted in Joachims (1998), Support Vector Machines (SVMs) are well suited for text categorisation. We have therefore used the LIBSVM (Chang and Lin, 2011) software, configured with the linear kernel function, to perform SVM classification for this work. A number of features can be used to construct a representative vector for each Tweet. For example ngrams (unigrams, bigrams or a combination of both), the number of words in the Tweet, the number of hash tags and hyperlinks used and the number of user mentions.

During the Tweet annotation process a couple of features stood out as being particularly important: firsthand reports are usually short, don't contain a hyperlink and often contain particular words including exclamations. It was unclear whether the other features would be helpful or not.

Note that that all Tweets used in the training process contained either the word 'earthquake' or the hash tag '#eqnz': these are the keywords currently monitored by the heuristic earthquake detector. These particular instances of unigram features should not contribute to the outcome.

To determine which features contribute to the

Table 1: Examples of positive and negative Tweets

Firsthand reports	Not firsthand reports
Woah! Earthquake	Magnitude 3.8 earthquake shakes Wellington: Wellingtonians were shaken awake by a magnitude 3.8 earthquake early... http://t.co/rT4UvjzH
Earthquake!! 2 small 3-second-each tremors just now!!	i thought there was an earthquake or some sort of world ending experience but then i realised my brother was running around upstairs.. woops
That was a goodun. #eqnz	Large earthquake struck Vanuatu. Imagine the thoughts running through their heads when the earth started to shake
oooh, big wobble, heard that coming way off #eqnz	Can't believe it's been 2 years today since Christchurch had its major earthquake #KiaKaha

task of identifying firsthand earthquake reports, a 10 fold cross validation process (Hastie et al., 2009) was used with all combinations of the following features: ngram combinations, Tweet length, hash tag count, user mention count and hyperlink count. Table 2 shows a subset of the results, including the accuracy measures achieved by training on each single feature only, plus the highest scoring feature combination.

Table 2: Training Results (averages)

Feature	Accuracy (% correct)	F1 score
Tweet length (word count)	77.9	0.796
User mention count	64.2	0.746
Hash tag count	65.8	0.654
Hyperlink count	73.1	0.800
Unigrams	86.7	0.882
Bigrams	80.7	0.843
Combo of uni and bigrams	86.5	0.880
Unigrams plus all others	90.3	0.912

As expected, the words used within each Tweet (ngrams), the hyperlink count and Tweet length all perform well by themselves, with the user mention count and hash tag count in particular being less important. The combination of all of these features however, produces the highest average accuracy and F1 score.

4.4 More Training Data

The combination that produced the best score in the feature selection process was used to train a classifier using the annotated Tweet data described in Section 4.2. It was not appropriate to use this classifier to revisit the accuracy of the earthquake alerts since the Tweets contributing to each alert were used to train the classifier. Instead, a new training dataset was created from Tweet data before December 2012; before the heuristic detector was deployed.

The classifier was used to aid this process. The Tweets contributing to historical earthquake alerts (pre December 2012) were processed by the classifier to generate roughly 2000 suggested positive and negative Tweets. As before, each suggested positive and negative Tweet was examined and incorrect labels were manually adjusted resulting in 1094 positive and 940 negative Tweets.

The classifier was then retrained over the new training data set using the same features identified earlier. Evaluation of the new classifier using the initial training data as the test set produced an accuracy of 91.13% and an F1 score of 0.921.

4.5 Removing Stop Words

When preparing Tweet ngrams for the classifier, stop words are removed. Our stop word list is similar to those commonly used for traditional Natural Language Processing (NLP) tasks. It has however been extended to include additional Twitter related words and expletives, which are commonly used when experiencing an earthquake event: removing them may reduce the effectiveness of the classifier.

Experiments were run to determine the accuracy of the classifier due to the stop word removal process. Three training and test runs were carried out with various stop words lists: the original list, the original list with expletives and exclamation words removed and an empty list.

The results, shown in Table 3, indicate that the classifier worked slightly better with a modified stop word list and slightly better again with no stop words. Based on this, all future experiments used an empty stop word list.

Table 3: Stop Word Combination Results

Stop word set	F1 score	Accuracy
original	0.9207	91.13%
modified	0.9221	91.19%
empty	0.9223	91.38%

4.6 Feature Selection Revisited

With a now larger collection of annotated Tweet data and evidence that stop word removal should not be used, the feature selection process was revisited. This time, instead of using the 10 fold cross validation process, a simple time-split validation process (Sheridan, 2013) was used: Tweets before a certain time are used to train the classifier and Tweets after are used for testing.

The same cut off time of mid December 2012 was used. In addition to the first set of features evaluated, the presence of a hash tag or mention was now included. This resulted in 144 iterations looking at all feature combinations.

The best performing combination found was unigrams, Tweet length, mention count and hyperlink count with an accuracy of 91.44% and an F1 score of 0.922. Note that in this case, higher accuracy results were achieved without the hash tag related features and unigrams once again outperformed bigrams.

4.7 Tweet Count for Training

Annotating large numbers of Tweets is an onerous process taking considerable time to accomplish. The dependence of the training set size to the accuracy of the resulting classifier was tested. This was done by repeatedly training and testing the classifier using training set sizes of 50, 100, 150 and so on. Initially we naively chose the first 50 Tweets from the training data based on their creation timestamps, and then included the next 50 and so on. The Tweets were selected in chronological order rather than random order to emulate increasing Tweet collection periods. The results are shown in Figure 3.

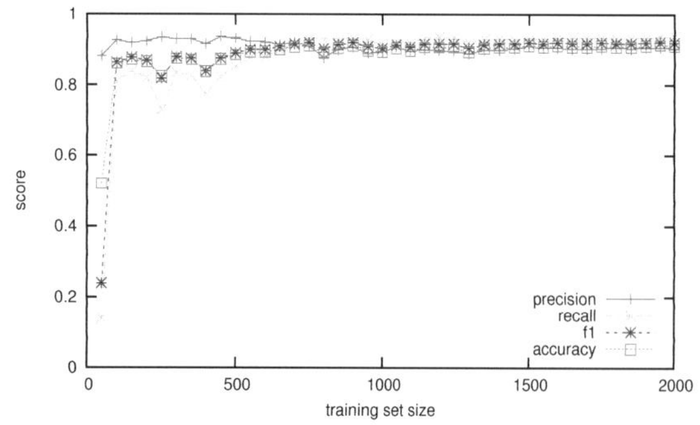

Figure 3: Accuracies: increasing training sizes

Figure 3 shows that almost the same accuracy (89.4% and F1 score of 0.903) can be achieved by annotating only 1000 Tweets which is half the size of our original training set. The variation in the results for smaller training set sizes was concerning. This may be due to a bias resulting from uneven proportions of positive and negative Tweets used. After examining the mix of Tweets used in these test sets, we found this was the case: there were only 71 positive Tweets in the test set of size 500.

To account for the variation in classifier performance over smaller training set sizes, we ran another experiment where we tried to evenly balance the proportion of positive to negative Tweets, where possible. The results are shown in Figure 4 where it can be seen that classifier performance improved significantly even for small data sets.

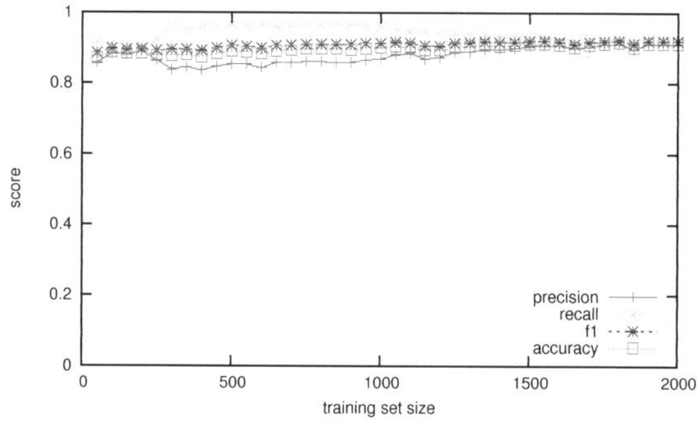

Figure 4: Accuracies: equal Tweet mix

5 Improved Earthquake Alerting

5.1 Summary

The classifier has now been trained on approximately 2000 Tweets from September 2010 to December 2012. It has been configured to use the features: unigrams, Tweet length, hyperlink count and mention count and does not perform stop word removal. Using this classifier, the Tweets contributing to the original post December 2012 earthquake alerts have been reanalysed. For each alert we now generate two additional statistics: the percentage of Tweets classified as positive and the geographic spread (*GeoSpread*) of just the positive Tweets. The *GeoSpread* measure is an indication of how close geographically a collection of Tweets is. This is one of the tests used in the existing heuristic detector and has values ranging from 1 (very close – in the same suburb) through to 15 (far apart – continental scale).

5.2 Further Improvements

When an earthquake alert has subsequent alerts within 30 minutes of the first, the next two alerts are also used to generate statistics. The aim was to determine if testing follow up alerts is helpful. There have been occasions when the first alert fails the heuristic detector's threshold criteria and is immediately followed by an alert that passes.

We evaluated the alerts using a variety of modifications to the original heuristic algorithm and with variations of classifier configuration. The results are shown in the Table 4.

5.3 Results

As can be seen from Table 4, adding the new rule where the percentage of positively classified Tweets must be at least 50% dramatically increases our F1 score. Also, it has removed all of the original false positive instances. Using the *GeoSpread* of only positively classified Tweets instead of all non-retweets also improved the result, although in our test cases it only removed one false negative instance.

Extending the evaluation to include the alert that immediately follows the original also improved the accuracy. However, in the cases where it is the second alert that passes the test, there is a delay of at least one minute before the notification is sent. This is due to the time taken to identify the second alert generated from the advancing buffer as described in Section 3.1. Evaluating the next two alerts did not improve the accuracy significantly; one false negative instance was removed but a new false positive instance was added.

The final test relaxed the rules for the minimum number of Tweets and the retweet percentage producing the highest F1 score and reducing the number of false negatives to 4, but an extra 2 false positives are introduced.

Overall, the use of a text classifier has greatly improved the accuracy of our earthquake detector, from the original F1 score of 0.667 to 0.881 and original accuracy of 89.87% to 96.85%.

5.4 Deployment

The inclusion of a text classifier has shown to significantly improve the accuracy of our detector. The contents of the notification email generated via the heuristic detector has been extended to include the classification results.

Figure 5 shows an example notification email. The first section contains a summary of the 'earthquake' alert noting the heuristic result that triggered the notification: the *GeoSpread* measures, retweet percentage and a classification summary. It also contains further information produced from our social media platform not previously discussed: the results of clustering the Tweets contributing to the alert and a summary of the Tweet locations.

```
red 'earthquak' alert generated at: Mon, 6 May 2013 14:20:18 +1000

Statistics:
  Number of tweets (including retweets): 59
  Retweets: 1.69%
  Geographic spread: 0.95

Results of running the "Firsthand earthquake 'felt' reports" classifier:
  Percentage of tweets classified as positive: 91.53%
  Geographic spread of positively classified tweets: 0.95

Location Summary (excluding retweets):
  Wellington (-41.28054,174.767136) - 40 tweets
  New Zealand (-43.586578,170.371384) - 11 tweets
  -41.2771551, 174.7774485 (-41.2771551,174.7774485) - 1 tweets
  Aro Valley (-41.296181,174.763046) - 1 tweets
  Petone (-41.221291,174.875076) - 1 tweets
  Upper Hutt (-41.12458,175.069031) - 1 tweets
  Christchurch (-43.531311,172.637299) - 1 tweets
  *unknown location - 2 tweets

Cluster Topics:
  Eqnz - 11 tweets
  Earthquake Wellington - 10 tweets
  Earthquakes - 3 tweets
  Wind - 3 tweets
  Building - 2 tweets
  Felt - 2 tweets
  Holy - 2 tweets
  Small - 2 tweets
  OMG - 2 tweets
  Other Topics - 33 tweets

Tweets (excluding retweets, +/- labels indicate classification result):
+ 06/05/2013 14:19:36 (Wellington, New Zealand) Oooh earthquake.
+ 06/05/2013 14:19:36 (Wellington) Earthquake!
+ 06/05/2013 14:19:37 (Wellington, New Zealand) Earthquake! #eqnz
+ 06/05/2013 14:19:37 (-41.2771551, 174.7774485) Earthquake?
- 06/05/2013 14:20:12 (Wellington New Zealand) eeeek.  As if the rain wasn't enough.....an earthquake thrown in.
- 06/05/2013 14:20:15 (Wellington, New Zealand) Earthquake?? Everyone round the office thinks so
- 06/05/2013 14:20:16 (Auckland/Christchurch, NZ) Earthquake, Magnitude 3.6, Monday, May 6 2013 at 4:19:11 pm,
30 km south-west of Martinborough http://t.co/xPPrizdjS2 #eqnz
```

Figure 5: Example notification email

The bottom section of the email summarises the Tweet content each prefixed by a '+' or '-' to indicate the classification result. Note that this example was generated by replaying an historical event and wasn't generated via live Tweet data. Also the list of Tweets has been edited to save space.

The information in the notification email performs three functions: it alerts the recipient of the possibility of an earthquake event, it provides a summary of the reasoning as to why an alert has been generated (the heuristics met and the text classifier results), and it includes a concise summary of the information reported on Twitter.

The reader of the email can quickly assess if the alert is genuine, a *true positive*, and determine the intensity of the earthquake with reference to the number of Tweets reported and by quickly reviewing their content.

6 Further Work

We are developing a classifier to determine an earthquake's intensity analogous to the MMI (Eiby, 1966). Examination of Tweets related to an earthquake reveals that a small percentage contain descriptions of the impact. For example the following (real) Tweet could be classified as level 'VI Strong' in the MMI scale:

Massive earthquake. House covered in glass. Bookshelf on floor. Lights fallen out. Still shaking

This information can be combined with demographic information to help in this determination: a small number of Tweets originating from a sparsely populated region would be given more

Table 4: Results

Modification	TP	FP	TN	FN	F1	accuracy	Heuristic rules used
Original heuristic	23	11	181	12	0.667	89.87%	numTweets > 3 geoSpread < 4 RT% < 18
Including classification	23	0	192	12	0.793	94.71%	numTweets > 3 geoSpread < 4 RT% < 18 pos% >= 50
Including classification and GeoSpread of positive Tweets	23	0	192	11	0.807	95.13%	numTweets > 3 posGeoSpread < 4 RT% < 18 pos% >= 50
Looking at next alert as well	25	0	192	7	0.877	96.88%	numTweets > 3 posGeoSpread < 4 RT% < 18 pos% >= 50 (for either alert 1 or 2)
Looking at next 2 alerts	25	1	191	6	0.877	96.86%	numTweets > 3 posGeoSpread < 4 RT% < 18 pos% >= 50 (for either alert 1 or 2 or 3)
Looking at the next 2 alerts with relaxed numTweets and RT% rules	26	3	189	4	0.881	96.85%	numTweets > 2 posGeoSpread < 4 RT% < 30 pos% >= 50 (for either alert 1 or 2 or 3)

'weight' compared to the same number of Tweets from a densely populated region. There are other opportunities around data integration also: combining with existing seismic sensor information and utilizing finer grained geo-location of Tweets.

There are also other areas to explore with our Social Media platform. The notification features will be extended to include other emergency management use cases such as fire detection and monitoring, cyclone tracking, flood events and crisis management incidents, for example terrorist attacks and criminal behaviour.

Another area of development is to use classifiers trained to identify impact information. Such classifiers, for example Yin et al. (2012), could be integrated with our system and we intend to experiment with different SVM configurations (error rates and kernel functions) and explore the use of semi-supervised learning using an inductive/transductive SVM to incrementally further train a classifier with user provided input as a 'live' event unfolds.

When an earthquake event is identified, subsequent Tweets could be processed by the impact classifiers to produce a follow up impact analysis email a short time afterwards.

7 Conclusions

Our social media platform provides information captured, filtered and analysed from Twitter using a background language model to characterise the 'normal' activity. Unusual events are identified as alerts when the observed activity varies from that historically recorded. These alerts are then filtered and the contributing Tweets processed to identify evidence of an actual earthquake event.

The initial heuristic based detector has been significantly improved by the introduction of a text classifier. The process of training the classifier has been extensively reported outlining the journey taken to identify different collections of test data, alternative methods of training the classifier, the impact of filtering stop words and the effect of varying the training set size when training the classifier.

The result has been been an incremental improvement to our ability to identify earthquake events as reported on Twitter. Our detector has improved in terms of the *F1 score* from an initial value of 0.667 to 0.881.

Our system generates email notifications of a possible earthquake event, summarises why our system considers it be evidence of firsthand 'felt' reports and includes a concise summary of the information from Twitter. The recipient can quickly assess if the alert is genuine and gain a quick overview of the intensity of the earthquake with reference to the number of Tweets reported and by reviewing their content.

Acknowledgments

Thanks to Daniel Jaksa (JATWC GA) who came up with the idea for a Twitter based MMI scale detector. Thanks also to our colleagues John Lingad, Sarvnaz Karimi and Jie Yin for developing the classification software that we used for our experiments and to David Ratcliffe who provided valuable feedback on the correct use of SVM.

References

Alliance Strategic Research. 2011. Social media in the 2011 victorian floods. Technical report, Office of the Emergency Services Commissioner and Victoria State Emergency Service, GPO Box 4356 Melbourne VIC 3001, June. [Accessed: 6 May 2013].

Martin Anderson. 2012. Integrating social media into traditional management command and control structures: the square peg into the round hole. In Peter Sugg, editor, *Australian and New Zealand Disaster and Emergency Management Conference*, pages 18–34, Brisbane Exhibition and Convention Centre, Brisbane, QLD. AST Management Pty Ltd.

Axel Bruns and Jean E. Burgess. 2012. Local and global responses to disaster: #eqnz and the christchurch earthquake. In Peter Sugg, editor, *Australian and New Zealand Disaster and Emergency Management Conference*, pages 86–103, Brisbane Exhibition and Convention Centre, Brisbane, QLD. AST Management Pty Ltd.

Axel Bruns, Jean Burgess, Kate Crawford, and Frances Shaw. 2012. #qldfloods and @QPSMedia: Crisis Communication on Twitter in the 2011 South East Queensland Floods. Technical report, ARC Centre of Excellence for Creative Industries and Innovation, QUT Z1-515, Musk Ave Kelvin Grove, Qld. 4059 Australia, January.

Mark A. Cameron, Robert Power, Bella Robinson, and Jie Yin. 2012. Emergency situation awareness from twitter for crisis management. In *Proceedings of the 21st international conference companion on World Wide Web*, WWW '12 Companion, pages 695–698, New York, NY, USA. ACM.

Chih-Chung Chang and Chih-Jen Lin. 2011. LIBSVM: A library for support vector machines. *ACM Transactions on Intelligent Systems and Technology*, 2:27:1–27:27. Software available at `http://www.csie.ntu.edu.tw/~cjlin/libsvm`.

Kym Charlton. 2012. Disaster management and social media - a case study. Technical report, Media and Public Affairs Branch, Queensland Police Service, GPO Box 4356 Melbourne VIC 3001. [Accessed: 26 April 2013].

Paul S. Earle, Daniel C. Bowden, and Michelle Guy. 2012. Twitter earthquake detection: earthquake monitoring in a social world. *Annals of GeoPhysics*, 54(6):708–715.

G. A. Eiby. 1966. The modified mercalli scale of earthquake intensity and its use in new zealand. *New Zealand Journal of Geology and Geophysics*, 9(1-2):122–129.

Trevor Hastie, Robert Tibshirani, and Jerome Friedman. 2009. *The elements of statistical learning: data mining, inference and prediction*. Springer, 2 edition.

Thorsten Joachims. 1998. Text categorization with suport vector machines: Learning with many relevant features. In *Proceedings of the 10th European Conference on Machine Learning*, ECML '98, pages 137–142, London, UK, UK. Springer-Verlag.

Bruce R. Lindsay. 2011. Social media and disasters: Current uses, future options, and policy considerations. Technical report, Analyst in American National Government, GPO Box 4356 Melbourne VIC 3001, September. `http://www.fas.org/sgp/crs/homesec/R41987.pdf`.

Marcelo Mendoza, Barbara Poblete, and Carlos Castillo. 2010. Twitter under crisis: Can we trust what we rt? In *Proceedings of the first workshop on social media analytics*, pages 71–79. ACM.

Qld Budget. 2011. Queensland Government: Budget Strategy and Outlook. page 66, March. [Accessed: 2013-04-9].

RBA. 2011. Reserve Bank of Australia: Statement on Monetary Policy. pages 36–39, February. [Accessed: 2013-04-9].

Bella Robinson, Robert Power, and Mark Cameron. 2013. A sensitive twitter earthquake detector. In *Proceedings of the 22nd international conference on World Wide Web companion*, WWW '13 Companion, pages 999–1002, Republic and Canton of Geneva, Switzerland. International World Wide Web Conferences Steering Committee.

Takeshi Sakaki, Makoto Okazaki, and Yutaka Matsuo. 2010. Earthquake shakes twitter users: real-time event detection by social sensors. In *Proceedings of the 19th international conference on World wide web*, WWW '10, pages 851–860, New York, NY, USA. ACM.

Takeshi Sakaki, Makoto Okazaki, and Yutaka Matsuo. 2013. Tweet analysis for real-time event detection and earthquake reporting system development. *IEEE Transactions on Knowledge and Data Engineering*, 25(4):919–931.

Robert P. Sheridan. 2013. Time-split cross-validation as a method for estimating the goodness of prospective prediction. *Journal of Chemical Information and Modeling*, 53(4):783–790.

Catherine Stephenson, John Handmer, and Aimee Haywood. 2012. Estimating the net cost of the 2009 black saturday fires to the affected regions. Technical report, RMIT, Bushfire CRC, Victorian DSE, February.

Sudha Verma, Sarah Vieweg, William J Corvey, Leysia Palen, James H Martin, Martha Palmer, Aaron Schram, and Kenneth M Anderson. 2011. Natural language processing to the rescue?: Extracting'situational awareness' tweets during mass emergency. *Proc. ICWSM*.

Jie Yin, Andrew Lampert, Mark Cameron, Bella Robinson, and Robert Power. 2012. Using social media to enhance emergency situation awareness. *IEEE Intelligent Systems*, 27(6):52–59.

Computer-assisted Structuring of Emergency Management Information: A Project Note

Yotaro Watanabe **Kentaro Inui**
Tohoku University
{yotaro-w,inui}@ecei.tohoku.ac.jp

Shingo Suzuki
Kyoto University
shingo@drs.dpri.kyoto-u.ac.jp

Hiroko Koumoto
Fuji Tokoha University
koumoto@fuji-tokoha-u.ac.jp

Mitsuhiro Higashida
ESIP
m-higashida@kansai-kumikomi.net

Yuji Maeda
NTT Secure Platform Laboratories
maeda.y@lab.ntt.co.jp

Katsumi Iwatsuki
Tohoku University
iwatuki@riec.tohoku.ac.jp

Abstract

In order to achieve high-level resilience against disasters, effective utilization of previous emergency management information is necessary. The goal of this project is to establish effective utilization of emergency management information and emergency response logs that are accumulated as a fundamental dataset to learn lessons for emergencies in the future. More precisely, we develop a framework that simplifies structuring emergency management information and creating databases through various media or formats by exploiting technologies such as natural language processing to fix the bottlenecks for inputting information in emergency response sites, to share disaster state, and to contribute towards achieving more effective use of human resources. The academic aim of this project is to establish the task of creating a database of emergency management information as a subfield of natural language processing applications.

1 Introduction

In order to confront natural disasters which could become a national crisis, high-level resilience against disasters is required. To achieve this, it is necessary to assume emergency situations, prompt actions for emergencies, and conduct quick and correct restorations and recoveries. This requires effective use of emergency management information.

In response to the 2011 Tohoku earthquake/tsunami in Japan, a strong desire for the development of new methods to improve emergency response came about. The basic framework for emergency management by local governments is the following: (i) As soon as a disaster takes place, the local government organizes a headquarter for disaster control, which consists of the mayor (as the director-general) and directors from executive branches (Water and Sewer Division, Civil Engineering Division, etc.) as well as representatives from the police, the fire station, etc. (ii) Each executive branch collects disaster information from a large variety of sources and responds to requests from disaster sites. (iii) The collected information is conveyed to the headquarter and also shared with other branches so that the headquarter and branches can effectively cooperate with each other. (iv) The headquarter keeps the situation in perspective and makes local government-wide decisions. (v) A summary of the accumulated disaster information and responses is communicated to neighboring local governments and the higher administrative division (i.e. prefecture or state).

As the reader may imagine from the above, the most important key for this whole system to work effectively is communication; i.e. the key issue is how efficiently and precisely information about the progress situation and the responses against it can be shared among the executive branches and the headquarter together with the outside of the disaster site. Unfortunately, however, the 3.11 earthquake revealed that in most local governments in the disaster-hit areas, the current means for emergency management communication was crucially inefficient, which sometimes caused miscommunications and prohibited the disaster control headquarters from making optimal or appropriate decisions. While the inefficiency of communication was partly due to severe damages of communication networks, critical problems arose even under the situation where communication networks were available. In most of the local governments in the disaster-hit areas, each piece of information from outside (through phone calls, radio communications, etc.) was recorded only

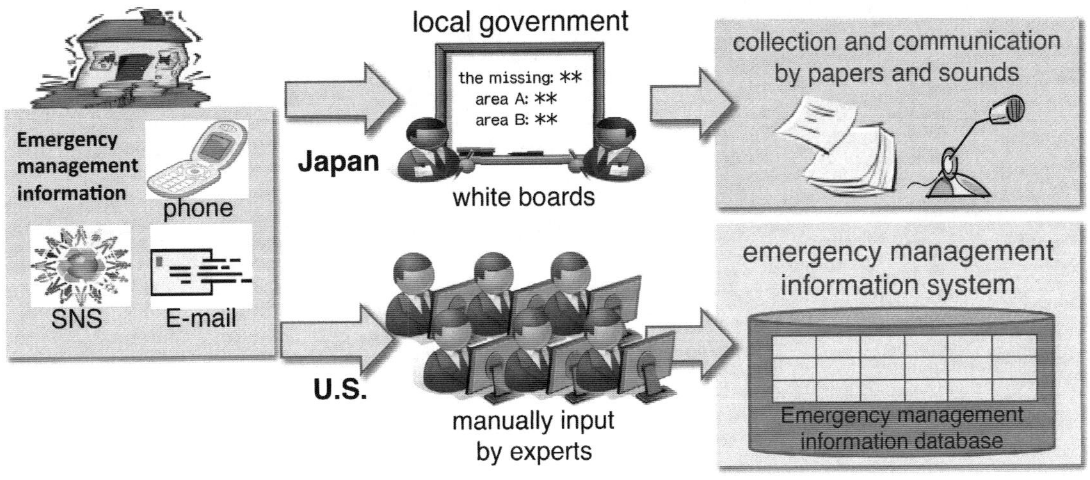

Figure 1: Emergency management systems in Japan and United States.

by hand writing and thus distributed to divisions in charge only by oral communication or through white boards as shown in Figure 1. This makes it difficult to efficiently share emergency management information among divisions and local governments, also hinders promptly update status of disaster response.

In contrast, in the United States, WebEOC (EOC: Emergency Operation Center), a web browser-based information system conformable to a standardization of incident management by NIMS (National Incident Management System), has been introduced to more than 80% of the state governments, and has achieved effective emergency responses. To operate the systems, professional employees are hired at each crisis management office to manually input emergency management information as structured information using a computer. Standardization of information management in crisis situations has internationally progressed and has been recommended for ISO 22320. On the other hand, such emergency management information systems have not been introduced to actual situations in Japan.

It is not enough that simply converting emergency management information from a large variety of sources to unstructured texts. Realizing quick and correct restoration and utilization of them for the future disasters needs making them as structured information to be searchable by storing, classifying and organizing them. The structurization consists of selecting one of database schemas and search its items from texts, and prohibitively high cost will be required if the operation is performed by human. In order to operate such system with limited resources, reducing the cost of structurization is essential.

Given this background, we have launched a government-founded three-year project to develop a system that assists with creating databases of emergency management information to digitize, accumulate and utilize them. We address the following three issues in this project.

Designing standard DB schemas for emergency management information By analyzing actual emergency response operations, we design standard DB schemas for emergency management information that can be commonly applied for diverse local governments.

Developing a system that assist with creating emergency management information databases By further advancement of natural language processing technologies, we develop a system that efficiently stores unstructured emergency management information to databases. This system at first extracts important information from unstructured texts, selects one of database schemas, and finally fills each of the elements with a corresponding expression in a text, as shown in Figure 2.

Environmental improvement for the usage of emergency management information systems We develop a training package that includes diverse and real scenario data and analyzes issues of developing information and communication technologies for emergency response through experi-

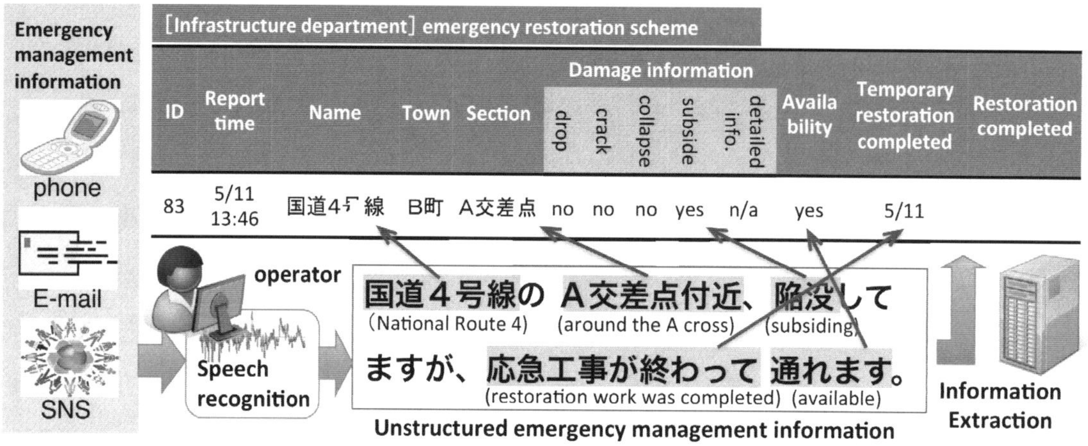

Figure 2: Creation of emergency management information databases.

ments of technologies of adding emergency management information to databases.

In addition, we develop a system that unifies these research outcomes and evaluates performance of the developed system by conducting experiments cooperated with the emergency management information system. Through discussions of technical and systematic issues we will have, we find knowledge for deploying the system into the field.

2 Research Issues and Plans in Our Project

In this project, we develop an emergency management information database creation support system using speech recognition and natural language processing technologies as shown in Figure 3. To do this, we (1) design emergency management information schemas, (2) develop an emergency management information database creation support system whose inputs consist of various forms of information such as speeches, faxes with handwritten characters, and so on, and (3) improve the environment for the usage of the emergency management information system. In addition, we incorporate the developed system into WebEOC, a standard emergency management information system, and then conduct demonstration experiments with the developed system by cooperating with local governments to analyze technical and systematic issues in deploying the system into the field. The detailed explanations of the tasks we address are explained as follows.

2.1 Task 1: Designing Emergency Management Information Schemas

In this task, we at first analyze emergency response operations thus far in local governments cooperating in this project. We then design and standardize emergency management information schemas and develop a system that assists with creating emergency management information databases. In addition, we develop a framework that automatically creates emergency management information in conjunction with WebEOC.

In our prior work, we developed a set of emergency management information schemas applicable to earthquake emergencies in local governments. In this project, we develop such schemas applicable for not only local governments, but also umbrella organizations of them, such as ordinance-designated cities and administrative divisions of Japan, and for central governments. In addition, we design a set of standardized schemas applicable for other emergency situations such as wind damage, flood damage, eruption and pandemics. In research and development, we not only clean up elements of emergency management information, but also extract and standardize them to be able to apply for several emergencies and local governments by analyzing results of demonstration experiments. More precisely, we first go to interview employees of disaster affected local governments. Next, we organize disaster response instances in chronological order by referring various forms of histories and analyze them to clear issues regarding emergency information processing. Because there are local governments who man-

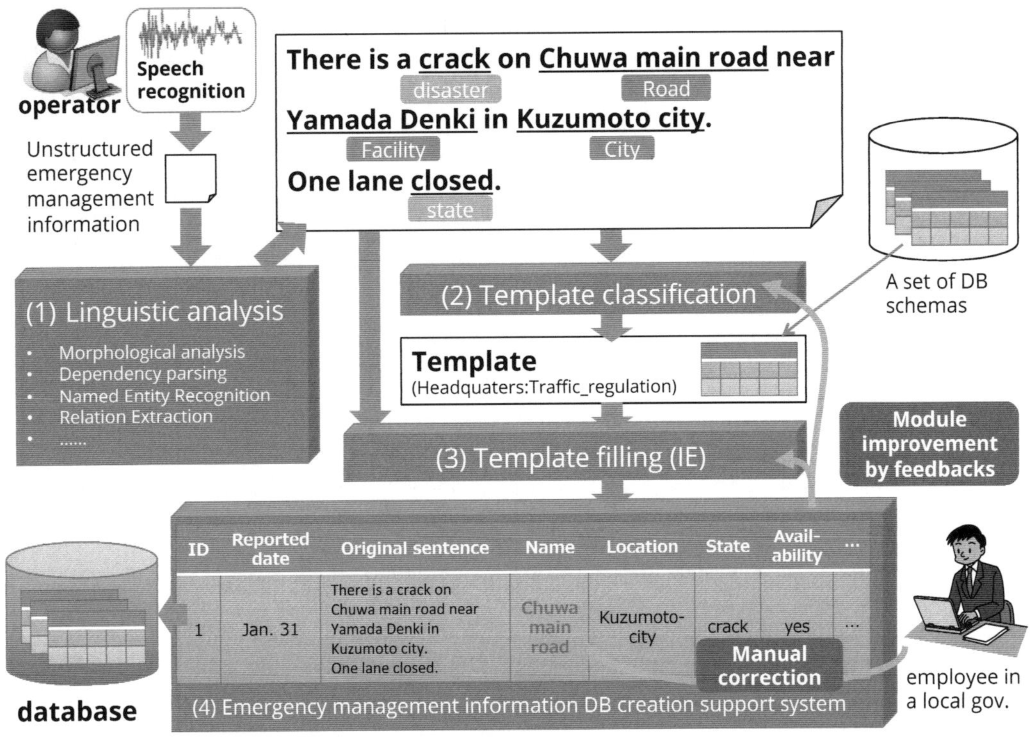

Figure 3: An emergency management information database creation support system.

age pieces of emergency information using paper-based media such as FAX and share them in their own formats as shown in Figure 4, we consider the needs for these local governments by establishing sharable and flexible emergency management information schemas customizable for each local government.

Then, we standardize emergency management information schemas through comparison to outcomes of previous work. Standardization of emergency management information schemas is conducted through several opportunities such as domestic or international conferences, and developed on a cloud-based system. For this, we develop a guideline of the cloud-based system as a emergency management cloud through ASPIC (ASP-SaaS-Cloud Consortium) [1] and encourage broad use of the system.

2.1.1 Research Issues and Plan

Toward efficient sharing of emergency responses, United States defined Incident Command System (ICS) Forms, a standard of federal emergency management, in which items required for ICS are defined. The templates of them were provided to WebEOC. However, it is unclear whether those forms are both necessary and sufficient for operating response activities. Additionally, they may not be applicable to response in Japan. In a Kashihara city case study, Higashida et al. (2012) created operational templates to deal with necessary data. Schemas of the templates indicate necessary data items for operations. They are, however, not based on information in actual response. In order to establish standard emergency management schemas which are applicable for various types of emergency situations and usable in ordinance-designated cities, the administrative divisions of Japan and central governments, we interview local governments to draw out information of past emergencies and analyze them to address the issue.

2.2 Task 2: Development of an Emergency Management Information Database Creation Support System

The task of developing an emergency management information database creation support system consists of (a) development of emergency management information structurization technologies and (b) development of a user interface for creating

[1] http://www.aspicjapan.org/

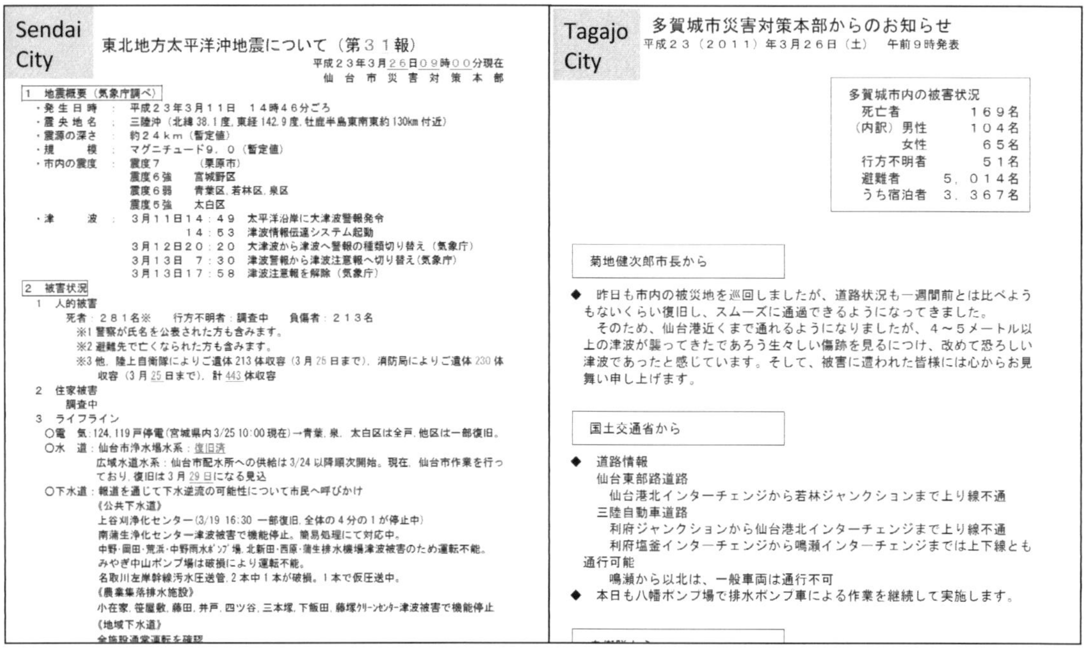
Sendai City
東北地方太平洋沖地震について（第３１報）
平成２３年３月２６日０９時００分現在
仙台市災害対策本部

1　地震概要（気象庁調べ）
・発生日時　：　平成２３年３月１１日　１４時４６分ごろ
・震央地名　：　三陸沖（北緯 38.1 度，東経 142.9 度，牡鹿半島東南東約 130km 付近）
・震源の深さ　：　約２４ｋｍ（暫定値）
・規模　：　マグニチュード９．０（暫定値）
・市内の震度　：　震度７　（栗原市）
震度６強　宮城野区
震度６弱　青葉区，若林区，泉区
震度５強　太白区
・津波　：　３月１１日１４：４９　太平洋沿岸に大津波警報発令
１４：５３　津波情報伝達システム起動
３月１２日２０：２０　大津波から津波へ警報の種類切り替え（気象庁）
３月１３日　７：３０　津波警報から津波注意報へ切り替え（気象庁）
３月１３日１７：５８　津波注意報を解除（気象庁）

2　被害状況
1　人的被害
死者：２８１名※　行方不明者：調査中　負傷者：２１３名
※1 警察が氏名を公表された方も含みます。
※2 避難先で亡くなられた方も含みます。
※3 他，陸上自衛隊によりご遺体 213 体収容（3 月 25 日まで），消防局によりご遺体 230 体収容（3 月 25 日まで），計 443 体収容
2　住家被害
調査中
3　ライフライン
○電　気：124，119 戸停電（宮城県内 3/25 10:00 現在）→青葉，泉，太白区は全戸，他区は一部復旧。
○水　道：仙台市浄水場水系：復旧済
広域水道水系：仙台市配水所への供給は 3/24 以降順次開始。現在，仙台市作業を行っており，復旧は 3 月 29 日になる見込
○下水道：報道を通じて下水逆流の可能性について市民へ呼びかけ
《公共下水道》
上谷刈浄化センター（3/19 16:30 一部復旧，全体の 4 分の 1 が停止中）
南蒲生浄化センター津波被害で機能停止。簡易処理にて対応中。
中野・岡田・荒浜・中野雨水ﾎﾟﾝﾌﾟ場，北新田・西原・蒲生排水機場津波被害のため運転不能。
みやぎ中山ポンプ場は破損により運転不能。
名取川左岸幹線汚水圧送管，2 本中 1 本が破損。1 本で仮圧送中。
《農業集落排水施設》
小在家，笹屋敷，藤田，井戸，四ツ谷，三本塚，下飯田，藤塚ｸﾘｰﾝｾﾝﾀｰ津波被害で機能停止
《地域下水道》
全施設通常運転を確認

Tagajo City
多賀城市災害対策本部からのお知らせ
平成２３（２０１１）年３月２６日（土）　午前９時発表

多賀城市内の被害状況	
死亡者	１６９名
（内訳）男性	１０４名
女性	６５名
行方不明者	５１名
避難者	５，０１４名
うち宿泊者	３，３６７名

菊地健次郎市長から

◆　昨日も市内の被災地を巡回しましたが、道路状況も一週間前とは比べようもないくらい復旧し、スムーズに通過できるようになってきました。
そのため、仙台港近くまで通れるようになりましたが、４～５メートル以上の津波が襲ってきたであろう生々しい傷跡を見るにつけ、改めて恐ろしい津波であったと感じています。そして、被害に遭われた皆様には心からお見舞い申し上げます。

国土交通省から

◆　道路情報
仙台東部路道路
仙台港北インターチェンジから若林ジャンクションまで上り線不通
三陸自動車道路
利府ジャンクションから仙台港北インターチェンジまで上り線不通
利府塩釜インターチェンジから鳴瀬インターチェンジまでは上下線とも通行可能
鳴瀬から以北は、一般車両は通行不可
◆　本日も八幡ポンプ場で排水ポンプ車による作業を継続して実施します。

Figure 4: Different forms of damage reports.

emergency management information databases.

2.2.1 Developing Emergency Management Information Structurization Technology

We assume that inputs in the system are digitized unstructured texts transformed from primary emergency management information such as sounds and papers, e-mails, and social networks. We develop a structurization technology that automatically extracts information which corresponds to items in schemas from unstructured texts.

Considering actual use of this technology, we have to handle not only text data but also speeches and images. However, considering the fact that this research has a limited time frame of only three years, we decided to concentrate on creating databases from digitized, unstructured texts. Since speech recognition performance depends on speech environment, acoustic model, etc., it is necessary to consider such factors into improve the accuracy of speech recognition which digitize emergency management information. In this project, we assume that speech input is performed by some particular operators. This enables us to provide invariable environment for speech recognition. Also we consider using a fixed form for reading out emergency management information. On the other hand, existing hand-written character recognition technologies are currently not reliable for use, so it would be necessary to read handwritten texts out loud and digitize the speech via speech recognition.

Structurizing emergency management information of digitized texts and converting them as databases can be seen as a task of information extraction. However, in contrast to the traditional information extraction tasks, our task is more complicated and challenging because there are diverse types of entries in emergency management information schemas to fill. For example, this task requires handling various types of information: not only named entities but also domain-specific events (subside, fire, etc.), modality information (e.g. available), etc. Since we have already developed several natural language processing technologies, we advance these technologies along with taking measures to adopt them for emergency management information. Also, as shown in Figure 2, various linguistic knowledge and domain knowledge are required to structurize emergency management information. For instance, we have to recognize that *a cross* represents a point in a road, the cross is located in a particular area, and "can pass through" means "the road is available". Thus exhaustive acquisition of such knowledge is critical to the successful development of this technology. We also advance investigating technologies of large-scale linguistic and domain knowledge acquisition from web pages.

2.2.2 Development of a User Interface of the Emergency Management Information Database Creation Support System

For the emergency management information databases we design in this project, we prepare schemas for more than ten divisions of local governments and define dozens of items for each of the schemas. The structurization we described in Section 2.2.1 requires extraction of extremely fine-grained database items from natural language text, and this kind of difficult task setting has not yet been explored in previous work. Thus, instead of using system outputs without change, we need a system which can easily display choices presented by the system for operators to select. To address this, we develop a high-quality framework that efficiently create databases from unstructured emergency management information by effectively using emergency management information structurization technologies. These technologies are improved through interactions with users and machine learning approaches which enable us to dynamically improve the performance of the system by user feedback.

2.2.3 Research Issues and Plan

The structurization includes diverse information extraction subtasks including named entity recognition (NER) such as location names (city, road, etc.), facility names (shelter, shop, school, etc.), numerical expression identification and normalizing, relation extraction (RE), location name disambiguation and slot filling.

In Message Understanding Conference (MUC) (Grishman and Sundheim, 1996) and Automatic Content Extraction (ACE) (Doddington et al., 2004) communities, various information extraction tasks including named entity recognition, relation extraction and slot filling have been explored. The task of disambiguation location expressions is called toponymy disambiguation, and has been explored by (Buscaldi and Rosso, 2008b; Buscaldi, 2010; Buscaldi, 2011; Habib and van Keulen, 2013; Bo et al., 2012; Lee et al., 2013) and GeoNLP Project[2]. For the task of disambiguation location names, Buscaldi and Rosso developed Geo-WordNet (2008a) in which entries of location names are coupled with their coordinates. TAC Knowledge Base Population (KBP) (McNamee and Dang, 2009; Ji et al., 2010a; Ji et al., 2010b) also has dealt with the task of entity disambiguation task as an entity linking problem where systems are required to link entity mentions to corresponding database entries. The difficulty of our task is that we have to detect fine-grained actual locations of location expressions which can include not only named entities but also expressions with general nouns (e.g. *the convenience store in front of the station*). Such disambiguation of general location expressions is a major issue since systems are required to predict actual entities from contextual information, etc. There is no previous work that addresses this kind of difficult task setting.

Also, how to collaborate with speech recognition systems is an important issue. Since the performance of the state-of-the-art speech recognition system is not perfect, we explore how to input emergency management information effectively and accurately from speeches.

Customizability is also an important requirement to make the system applicable for various local governments because processes of emergency management information can be different for each local government. We establish effective customizing methods through cooperating with local government employees.

2.3 Task 3: Environment Improvement for the Usage of Emergency Management Information Systems

In the Great East Japan Earthquake in 2011, it was indicated that emergency response requires information sharing between departments or organizations. In order to implement cross-organizational information sharing in disasters, it is essential to regularly hold emergency drills. Regarding drills, Hu et al. (2007) developed techniques for municipal employees to create drill scenarios reflecting local characteristics, by using samples. Motoya et al. (2009) examined emergency training management systems considering human resources development. The previous studies, however, were not focused on scenario contents which enable officials to enhance information sharing skills. It is essential in disasters to collect and handle information, create common operational pictures, and use them. Drill scenarios are required to check and

[2] `http://agora.ex.nii.ac.jp/GeoNLP/`

improve such skills. It is important to best utilize practical response data of the Earthquake to create such scenarios and implement drills to provide them.

For improvement of the environment for the usage of emergency management information systems, we prepare manuals that describe usage of the emergency management information systems and the database schemas used in the system. Also, we develop a scenario dataset for emergency drills. More precisely, we generate (a) hazard and damage maps for the purpose of training in emergency situations using a Web service we have developed. In addition, we create (b) a progress scenario of issues to be addressed based on the emergency management manuals, responses for flood damages, research results regarding cause-effect structures and the interview for employees in disaster affected local governments. Based on (a) and (b), we create a drill scenario dataset while appropriately including emergency responses for several emergency situations. Since we use the emergency management information database creation support system in training, we conduct situation annotation by using appropriate media consistent with the input interface of the system. Also, the drill scenario dataset will be used as a data for developing several structurization technologies in Task 2. To exploit the drill scenario data, we make the dataset capable, especially in size, for training machine learning models. This scenario dataset will also be used as an evaluation scenario for conducting demonstration experiments. In addition, we prepare a useful manual that describes the usage of the scenario dataset by clarifying required contents of the manual in the demonstration experiments.

2.3.1 Research Issues and Plan

In the improvement of the environment for the usage of emergency management information systems, we need emergency response data to develop drill scenarios. However, so far, digitized emergency responses have not been accumulated as archives. The records of emergency responses in Tohoku earthquake/tsunami have especially not been digitized, which can be effectively utilized to conduct emergency response training for potential Nankai Trough off the coast of western Japan. Developing training datasets and designing emergency management systems require actual emergency management records that are digitized and recorded in a unified way. However, there are several local governments which cannot provide such records. In order to address this issue, we develop a drill scenario data by enhancing limited emergency response data obtained from interviews for emergency responders by complementing them with damage information and status information. In addition, we take every possible means to develop drill scenario data by examining media used for situation annotation and considering status change due to emergency responses. After the development, we improve the data by asking employees in charge of disasters in local governments to check the data. By developing a multiple drill scenarios, we make the data applicable for various local governments.

To encourage broad use of the system, we demonstrate the system and conduct emergency response training in the local governments that cooperated with us. In the encouragement, we make the system cloud-based and construct a system which makes it easily available to conduct training in local governments through networks. In making the system cloud-based, we follow ISO22320, the standard of emergency management.

3 Current Status

We have already developed cooperative relations with some disaster affected local governments and have analyzed emergency response records provided by them in regards to how many contacts were received for each division, etc. From the analysis, we obtained fundamental information which should be considered in the development of database schemas. By analyzing the documents of the emergency management headquarter, we found that (i) updates of emergency information are mainly focused on 3 days after the disaster and (ii) understanding an overview of the disaster is easily accomplished by organizing and fixing items of emergency management information beforehand, etc.

Based on the data and the analysis, we developed a sample scenario data consisting of 100 entries and used it as reference data for designing the system. Table 1 shows some entries extracted from the developed scenario data.

Based on the data, we analyzed the task of creating emergency management information databases in the light of natural language processing, and designed a flow consisting of structur-

Affairs division	Text
本部:消火活動 Headquarters:Extinguishing	17 時現在、15 時に発生した洞沢の火災は鎮火しました。 The fire occurred at 3 p.m. in Dozawa was extinguished.
本部:物資調達 Headquaters:Procurement	ベビーおむつの在庫が支所にはありません。中上薬局から粉ミルクも確保する必要があります。 Diaper is now out-of-stock in the branch. It is also necessary to obtain the powder milk from Nakaue pharmacy.
本部:交通規制対応 Headquarters:Traffic_regulation	大谷の国道４５線は津波によって陥没しており、通行不能です。 Route 45 in Otani is currently not available because there is subsidence due to tsunami.
避難所:開設・閉鎖 Shelter:Establishment/closing	小泉中の避難所を副分団長が確認しました。昨日より開設とのこと。電気もガスも水も使えないので支援願います。 The vise-reader of the division checked a shelter in Koizumi junior high school. It has been established from yesterday. Utilities are not available. Support is requested.
避難所:施設復旧 Shelter:Restoration	津谷中学校は、停電していますが、教室を解放して避難者を受け入れています。 There is no electricity in Tsuya junior high school, but it is opening classrooms and accepting refugees.
避難所:物資 Shelter:Goods	寺谷からおにぎりが１００個の到着したので、仙翁寺にいる約２００人の消防団へ届けました。 We received 100 rice balls arrived from Teraya and sent them to a fire company which consists of about 200 members in Sennoji.
避難所:仮設トイレ Shelter:Temporary_lavatory	小泉中学校です。至急、10 個ほど仮設トイレを設置できないでしょうか？ This is Koizumi junior high school. Please install about 10 temporary bathrooms as soon as possible.
とりまとめ様式・避難者 Summary:Refugees	避難者の報告です。小泉中学校が約４００人、はまなすの丘が約３００人になります。 A report on refugees. There are about 400 refugees in Koizumi junior high school and about 300 refugees in Hamanasu-no Oka.

Table 1: Samples of the developed entries of emergency management information.

ization of natural language texts, template selection, information extraction, and error correction by humans. In the structurization of natural language texts, we found that we need morphological analysis, chunking, dependency parsing, coordination analysis, entity extraction, event extraction, numerical expression recognition, location expression recognition, relation extraction, modality analysis, voice analysis, aspect analysis, existence analysis, clause relation analysis, discourse relation analysis and anaphora resolution.

We have started to develop linguistic analyzers required for the development of the proposed system, including a numerical expression recognizer, location expression recognizer, relation extractor, etc. As of now, the developed system is still in infant stage.

4 Conclusion

In this paper, we described an overview of our project, developing a system that assists structuring of emergency management information, and its current status. To utilize emergency management information in order to improve resilience against emergencies, we develop a framework that simplifies structuring emergency management information through various media or formats by exploiting natural language processing technologies. The tasks we address in this project are: (1) Designing standard DB schemas for emergency management information, (2) Developing a system that assists with creating emergency management information databases, and (3) Environmental improvement for the usage of emergency management.

In the future, we plan on establishing the database schemas commonly applicable for various local governments, and we progress with the development of the system that assists with creating databases with emergency management information using natural language processing technologies. After the development, we include the developed system into WebEOC, a standard emergency management information system, and conduct demonstration experiments with local governments to analyze technical and systematic issues for deploying the system into the field.

References

Han Bo, Paul Cook, and Timothy Baldwin. 2012. Geolocation prediction in social media data by finding location indicative words. In *Proceedings of COLING 2012: Technical Papers*, pages 1045–1062.

Davide Buscaldi and Paolo Rosso. 2008a. Geowordnet: Automatic Georeferencing of wordnet. *Proc. LREC, Marrakech, Morocco.*

Davide Buscaldi and Paolo Rosso. 2008b. Map-based vs. knowledge-based toponym disambiguation. In *Proceedings of the 5th ACM Workshop On Geographic Information Retrieval (GIR 2008)*, pages 19–22.

Davide Buscaldi. 2010. *Toponym disambiguation in information retrieval*. Ph.D. thesis, .

Davide Buscaldi. 2011. Approaches to disambiguating toponyms. *SIGSPATIAL Special*, 3(2):16–19, July.

George R. Doddington, Alexis Mitchell, Mark A. Przybocki, Lance A. Ramshaw, Stephanie Strassel, and Ralph M. Weischedel. 2004. The Automatic Content Extraction (ACE) Program - Tasks, Data, and Evaluation. In *Proceedings of LREC 2004*.

Ralph Grishman and Beth Sundheim. 1996. Message understanding conference-6: A brief history. In *Proceedings of the 16th conference on Computational linguistics - Volume 1*, COLING '96, pages 466–471.

Mena B Habib and Maurice van Keulen. 2013. A Hybrid Approach for Robust Multilingual Toponym Extraction and Disambiguation. In *International Conference on Language Processing and Intelligent Information Systems, LP & IIS 2013*.

Mitsuhiro Higashida, Masahiro Sugiyama, Hideki Takeda, Tomomi Yamamoto, Yuji Maeda, and Haruo Hayashi. 2012. Analysis of information processing patterns appeared at emergency operation center training. *Outline of Social Safety and Science*, 30:93–96.

Zhexin Hu, Yasunori Hada, Toyoharu Itou, and Yashushi Saitou. 2007. A study on scenario making methods for disaster response exercised by local government personnel. *Journal of Social Safety and Science*, 9:271–278.

Heng Ji, Ralph Grishman, Hoa Trang Dang, Kira Griffitt, and Joe Ellis. 2010a. Overview of the TAC 2010 knowledge base population track.

Heng Ji, Ralph Grishman, Hoa Trang Dang, Kira Griffitt, and Joe Ellis. 2010b. Overview of the TAC 2011 knowledge base population track.

Kisung Lee, Raghu Ganti, Mudhakar Srivatsa, and Prasant Mohapatra. 2013. Spatio-Temporal Provenance: Identifying Location Information from Unstructured Text. In *IEEE Information Quality and Quality of. Service for Pervasive Computing (IQ2S)*.

Paul McNamee and Hoa Trang Dang. 2009. Overview of the TAC 2009 knowledge base population track.

Yutaka Motoya, Haruo Hayashi, Norio Maki, Keiko Tamura, Reo Kimura, and Kayoko Takemoto. 2009. Suggestions on how to design efficient training and management systems for personnel in charge of emergency responses, placing an emphasis on the process of developing human resources: A study based on the development and operation of the personnel training system designed for the cabinet office's division in charge of disaster prevention. *Journal of Social Safety and Science*, 11:203–213.

Rescue Activity for the Great East Japan Earthquake Based on a Website that Extracts Rescue Requests from the Net

Shin Aida
Toyohashi University of Technology
Aichi, Japan
aida@cs.tut.ac.jp

Yasutaka Shindo
Free
ring@quruli.ivory.ne.jp

Masao Utiyama
National Institute of Information and Communications Technology
Kyoto, Japan
mutiyama@nict.go.jp

Abstract

At the early phase of the Great East Japan Earthquake a vast number of tweets were made on Twitter. Even though many of them were calling for emergency rescue, they were not found timely due to the vast number of tweets including well-intentioned tweets to support those emergency rescues. In order to deal with the situation, the authors developed and launched a website on March 16, 2011, which automatically extracts rescue requests, categorizes similar statements into several statements and then lists them. This paper covers in detail not only the technology of the system but also how it has already collaborated and been applied to `#99japan`, a project to support delivering emergency rescue requests. Note that `#99japan` is an activity to monitor the process of the rescue based on Twitter and coming from the thread started by temporary volunteers who organized on a Japanese textboard 2 ちゃんねる "*2channel*."

1 Introduction

The Great East Japan Earthquake occurred on March 11, 2011 has obviously caused a wide range of damages. At the early phase of the earthquake, a large number of transmissions of information were made not only through mass-media in existence such as TV broadcast, newspaper and magazines but also social media such as Twitter. While the leading mass-media companies focused on information about the seriousness and damages due to the earthquake at affected areas for general public, the information which is useful for disaster survivor were also absolutely imperative. Under this situation, local radio broadcast, local newspaper and social media contributed to satisfy the needs.

From the early phase of the earthquake, a vast number of the tweets with the hashtag '`#j_j_helpme`', meaning requesting rescues, were made on Twitter, one of the most famous social media in Japan. These kinds of tweets included 【拡散希望】 "[Want to spread the information]", so that well-intentioned people who just wanted to contribute to help people highly tended to retweet those tweets unconditionally. As the result, similar rescue requests were flowed on Twitter and this made it very difficult to trace whether the rescue requests were actually reported to relevant authorities, which is the most important process.

In order to deal with the situation, we developed a website on March 15, 2011, which automatically extracts rescue requests, categorizes similar statements into several statements and then lists them and launched the website on the next day (Aida *et al.*, 2011; Aida *et al.*, 2013). This paper covers in detail not only the technology of the system but also how it has already collaborated and been applied to `#99japan`, a project to support delivering emergency rescue requests. Note that `#99japan` is an activity to monitor the process of the rescue based on Twitter and coming from the thread started by temporary volunteers who organized on a Japanese textboard 2 ちゃんねる "*2channel*".

2 Rescue Requests

2.1 Identification of Rescue Requests

We analysed the vast number of rescue requests in the early stages of the earthquake on Twitter; as a result, we identified the following four cases:

1. *Primary rescue request information*;
2. *Secondary rescue request information*, including redundant information;
3. *Non-rescue request information*; and
4. *Rescue completion report*.

We call information categorized in the case 1 or 2 *rescue requests* and one in the case 3 *a non-rescue request* respectively. Information categorized in the case 2 also includes a statement that contains the string 【拡散希望】 "[Want to spread the information]." Volunteers might not know whether or not each request was reported to authorities at each information; however, they still understood the current situation in the disaster area from a remote location by spread requests. Primary rescue requests on Twitter correspond to original tweets by some survivor and each secondary ones correspond to retweet, reply or mention.

On Twitter, it should be noted that statement is preceded by a time series back from the beginning of a sentence, where each quoted statement is postfix, and the primary rescue request is shown at the last place of the tweet in many cases:

> <u>**user1**</u>: `a mention for user2; RT @user2: a mention for user3; RT @user3 ... RT @usern: a primary rescue request.`
>
> *posted at* **MM/DD/YYYY hh:mm:ss**

2.2 Rescue Requests

In order to extract rescue requests on Twitter, we tried to find the words below that tended to be included in rescue requests, categorized them, and then summarized them as regular expressions in heuristics:

1. Rescue requests should include the following:
   - Words included in street addresses in order to identify the address of the rescue request (5 words).
   - Words related to the safety confirmation and to circumstances of life lines (21 words).

     Example: 消息 "whereabouts," 深刻 "serious," 要請 "request," 避難 "evacuation."

2. Non rescue requests should include the following:
   - Proper names that have been included in the past false rumours (14 words).

     Example: 花山村 "Hanayama village," which became Kurihara city merged with other surrounding municipalities in 2005, so it did not exist in 2011.
   - Official Twitter account names of the news media, because the media has almost already reported to relevant authorities (20 words).

     Examples: `radio_rfc_japan`, `fct_staff`, `[Aa]sahi`, `FKSminpo`, `[Nn][Hh][Kk]`, `nhk_seikatsu`, `i_jijicom_eqa`, `kahoku_shimpo`, `akt_akita_tv`, `NTV`, `telebee_tnc`, `NISHINIPPON`, `zakdesk`, `781fm`.
   - Specific person's names, such as celebrities and politicians, countries, party names and organization names, because there is no possibility of rescue requests including the thought and creed (9 words).

     Examples: 民主党 "Democratic Party of Japan," 自民党 "Liberal Democratic Party of Japan," 社民党 "Social Democratic Party," 共産党 "Communist Party,"
   - The names of countries and international organizations, because they are almost secondary information of the news media (6 words).

     Examples: アメリカ "USA," フランス "France," 国連 "United Nations," ユニセフ "UNICEF."
   - Words related to the nuclear accident, because rescue requests are not include scientific technical terminology (10 words).

     Examples: セシウム "cesium," ヨウ素 "iodine," ウラン "uranium," プルトニウ

ム "plutonium," 放射線 "radiation," 放射能 "radioactivity."

- Words unused in rescue requests (8 words).
  Examples: 笑 "laughing," 批判 "criticism," テロ "terrorism."
- Words included in tweets using too many hashtags, because they are independent of the original meaning of the tags (6 words).
  Examples: 予測市場 "forecasts market," リスクマネジメント情報 "risk management information."

3 Listing Policy for Rescue Requests

In the early stages of the earthquake, because we needed to release immediately our site extracting rescue requests, we decided to dare to volume display their requests on a single page in order for users not to look over information that they needed due to the info glut. Our site has been displayed 300 requests initially but now displayed 1000 requests at one time.

There were two reasons why we adopted the policy as listed below:

1. Extracted requests might include noise information. If we tightened filtering rules by our regular expression, it would be possible that the serious rescue requests would not be displayed.

2. By displaying rescue requests on the same page, volunteers could search requests in default feature of any web browser and, furthermore, avoid from checking multiple pages due to pagination.

Based on this policy, we manufacture a system extracting rescue requests by way of trial March 15, 2011, and launched the website on the next day (Aida *et al.*, 2011).

3.1 Extraction Algorithm of Rescue Request Information

Overview of the method of extraction algorithm of rescue request information on Twitter is as follows:

1. Obtain HTMLs on the tweet information including each search word listed in Figure 1 which is related to the earthquake disaster.

2. Perform the following process for all information obtained:

   (a) Merge tweets included in the HTMLs into the existing log file of the site and store the merged log file.

   (b) Preclude what appears to be non-rescue request information from the extracted log file by filtering according to the rules described in Section 2.2

   (c) Produce a *similar tweet key* by the following procedure based on the result of (b):

      i. Remove the longest string of up to "@" from the beginning of a tweet sentence.

      ii. Convert a similar tweet key into 15 letters obtained by removing the Japanese syllabary and ASCII characters.

   (d) Classify tweets into equivalent tweet classes, where we call the oldest tweet in equivalent class *represented tweet*, by using an associative array of similar tweet keys.

3. Make a list of latest 1000 items including the following lines and update the site:

   - Sentence of a represented rescue request tweet;
   - Tweet latest date and time of the tweet;
   - Tweet oldest date and time of the tweet:
   - The number of tweets in class including the tweet; and
   - Estimated source URL in the form "`http://twitter.com/screen_name/statuses/tweet_ID`".

4 Rescue Activity

In web-based rescue activities, volunteers needed to share situations about rescue activities. After our site opened, we scouted out for such activities to cooperate the site and really participated in a rescue activity `#99japan` organized by Kaichi Tamiya.

```
#j_j_helpme #j_i_helpme #hinan
#jishin #jisin #tunami
#311sppt #311care #311sien
#itaisousaku 99japan #anpi
#aitai #Funbaro #hope4japan
#prayforjapan #ganbappe
#save_busshi #save_volunteer
#save_gienkin #save_kids
#saigai #shinsai #tasukeai
#fukkou #fukko #save_miyagi
#save_fukushima #save_iwate
#save_aomori #save_ibaraki
#save_chiba #save_nagano
#save_sendai #save_ishinomaki
#save_iwaki #ishinomaki
#shiogama #rikuzentakata 緊
急地震 余震 火事 怪我 負傷者自宅避難
避難所 孤立 餓死 緊急+救助 食料+不足
物資+不足 食糧+不足 救援 支援 安否
消息 栄村 陸前高田釜石 大船渡 気仙沼
南三陸 歌津 志津川 石巻 松島 亘理 山
元 相馬 いわき 飯舘
```

Figure 1: Search Words to Extract Rescue Requests

4.1 Situation on the Net of In the Early Stages of the Great East Japan Earthquake

In the early stages of the earthquake, many activities have been launched in the Net. Disaster information has been made public in portal sites such as Yahoo! and Google.

In particular, "Google Person Finder" was well-known safety as confirmation system, which was used from the Haiti earthquake of January 2010 (Google, 2011). "ANPI NLP" was a project launched by voluntary researchers to augment the safety information of the system from the Net in a method of natural language processing (Murakami *et al.*, 2011; Neubig *et al.*, 2011).

As a system including rescue operations, "sinsai.info" was also well-known (Seki *et al.*, 2011). The site was constructed using a crowdsourcing tool *Ushahidi*, which was used in many disasters since 2007 and was famous as a system built on the day of the earthquake. Also, a variety of systems were published such as sites displaying a time line of tweets related to the earthquake tags on Twitter, radiation dose maps and so on.

However, countless volunteers and systems across the country could not quickly cooperate necessarily in the early stage; rather, utilizing existing systems, volunteers had decided the rules by trial and error and was involved in rescue activities.

In textboard *2channel*, the thread on rescue activities (*2channel*, 2011) was opened immediately in the day of the earthquake, Some anonymous volunteers participated in the thread launched a Wiki (*2channel* ID:nx64KwTT, 2011) and a rescue map (`#99japan`, 2011a) on the earthquake.

4.2 Rescue Assistance Project for The Great East Japan Earthquake: `#99japan`

March 15, 2011, Kaichi Tamiya (Twitter ID: `@ktamiya`) was managing a report activity history by using the comments section of his blog (Tamiya, 2011a). March 18, inviting members our rescue support activities taking advantage followers on Twitter, he organized *'the rescue assistance project for The Great East Japan Earthquake* `#99japan`" (Tamiya, 2011b).

Overview of this project activity was as follows:

- **目的:** Twitter 等での救助要請の声を適正機関に伝達する支援を行い，被災者を救う．

  Purpose: We notify agencies about the rescue requests obtained from the Net, such as Twitter, to save the survivors.

- **活動内容:** 主に被災者の情報の整理，内容確認，アドバイス，救助要請の代行．期間は物資が行き渡り，復興段階に入る頃までを予定．

  Activities: We report of rescue requests, verify the accuracy of request information and advice for survivors, until request supplies prevail in disaster-stricken areas and the areas enter the first stages of recovery.

This project adopted an existing editing rule for the rescue request map (`#99japan`, 2011a) and a supply request map (`#99japan`, 2011b), which were based on Google maps. In addition administrators of the maps also participated in `#99japan`, so it was notable that `#99japan` was one of the rescue projects for survivors in the early phase of the Great East Japan Earthquake.

`#99japan` was also a *hashtag on Twitter* as well as a project name. Any member of

#99japan could tweet many rescue requests and related activities appended with #99japan on Twitter, so their tweets shared among members. Of course, their tweets were also visible in the non-members. It was the biggest feature to communicate among users by the hashtag #99japan in the Twitter-based activities.

We proposed using our site to volunteers of #99japan to find rescue requests on the Net efficiently.

4.3 Activity Flow

We show below the activity flow of information sharing, map editing and source verification in #99japan (@ma_ chiman, 2011):

- Information sharing and map editing:
    1. Member of the project tweets rescue request information with a street address obtained by our site or other information sources, to which are appended the string "#99japan" as a hashtag in order to facilitate to share information to the members in a short period of time.
    2. According to of the shared information, member selects a point of the street address on the map and reports to relevant organizations such as the police, where the point is classified into
        (a) not reported;
        (b) reported but unknown whether resolved;
        (c) resolved already; or
        (d) other.
    3. Member fills in the content of report to the pop-up point in the map in a description rules.
- Source verification work:
    1. To update the local information that is constant number of days elapsed from the time of the rescue request, member follow the information providers and ask the change of environment.
    2. Member contacts the neighbourhood residents, asks their situation and writes a checking status to the map.
    3. Depending on the content and the presence or absence of reply, member reflects the following information on the pop-up of the point at the map:
        (a) resolved;
        (b) there is no new information;
        (c) not contact; or
        (d) other information,

        which are added the modified date and Twitter ID of reporting member.

4.4 Cooperative Rescue Activities with #99japan and Our Site

We continued to improve the site after the date as March 20 to conform to the needs of members.

We show a line graph about the number of accesses to the site as Figure 2. Analyzing the graph,

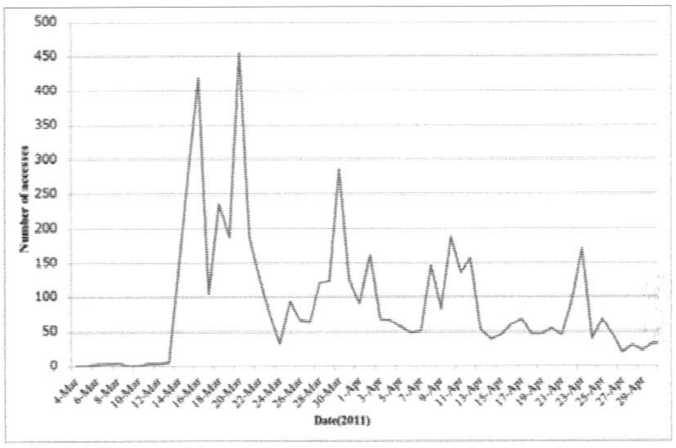

Figure 2: Changes in the Number of Accesses Our Site Extracting Rescue Requests.

we have confirmed the following trends:

- The number of accesses was particularly high activity immediately after the start of March 20 and the release date.
- Early April emerged from an emergency state, the number of accesses was increased temporarily.
- When large afterquakes was invoked in Miyagi April 4 and Fukushima of April 11 and 12 respectively, the number of accesses was increased again.

There was no quantitative data to show whether our site was helpful. Because most of the project members at the time is the anonymous participant, it is too difficult for our site to survey efficiency of rescue. However, we got good evaluated tweets on Twitter by the project #99japan chair Tamiya, @ma_chiman who opened the official website (@ma_ chiman, 2011) of the project, and the rescue map (#99japan, 2011a) administrator @juntaro33 as follows:

- Immediately after organizing #99japan, @ma_chiman suggested that the project members used our site to find rescue requests. (March 20, 2011.)
- When we implemented several additional functions into our site, @ma_chiman and @juntaro33 admire our implementation. (March 25, 2011.)
- @juntaro33 said that he was using our site as the most useful now. (April 2, 2011.)
- @juntaro33 said that most of the information on the map were obtained from our site. (April 6, 2011.)

By the project activity used the rescue map and the supply request map (Figure 3), The project had reporting and supporting activities more than 200 points on the rescue and supply request maps, respectively, in about three weeks until early April.

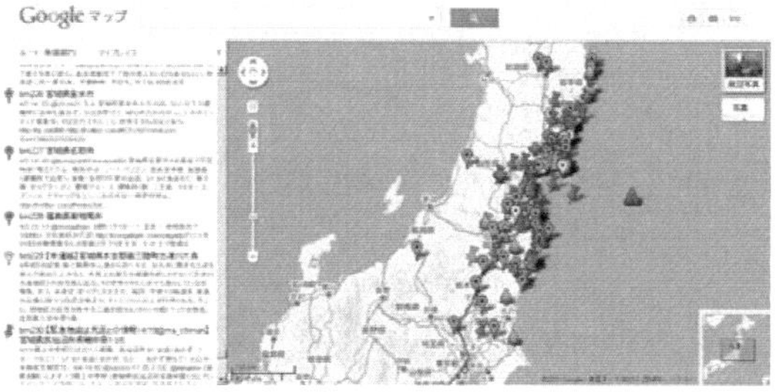

Figure 3: The Supply Request Map of #99japan.

5 Consideration for Our Actively

Looking back on #99japan, it was important to have *2channel* textboard as a virtual place to gather in case of large earthquake existed. In fact, *2channel* users became volunteers and shared disaster information such as rescue requests on the day of the earthquake on several social media, such as Twitter, mixi which was a famous SNS in Japan, Wiki sites and so on.

Then, Twitter users and others naturally joined the #99japan and they could share more rescue requests on Twitter. In particular, utilizing "#99japan" as a hashtag was a very significant as a mechanism that could be shared rescue progress and completion report. Importance of progress and completion report like this has been pointed out by many researchers on Twitter (Yamazaki *et al.*, 2012).

In the rescue activities, "freshness of the rescue request information" was particularly important; our site had contributed to the report activities support efficient, utilized as a source of information sources to #99japan.

6 Conclusion and Future Work

We developed and launched a website which extracted and listed rescue requests among all the information on Twitter on March 16, 2011, which was right after the Great East Japan Earthquake.

Through participating and collaborating with the activities of #99japan, a relief project of the Great East Japan Earthquake based on Twitter, it has turned out that exchanging messages to find appropriate information, report and check the status of the process on a timely basis based on the information of rescue requests listed on the website.

According to the requests of the members of #99japan, we also made efforts in order to increase the precision of extraction of information of rescue requests and to improve functions of the website for that. It is reported that social media was taken advantage of in backup activities at the early phase after the earthquake.

Further research could be analyzing the needs among the log file of the website which is still processing at present, and creating a well adaptive system for the disaster recovery relief.

It should be also noted that fortunately several important factors got connected by chance in #99japan. However it is also important to refine a framework of social system for letting volunteers work effectively and rapidly at disasters and at following restriction activities now in normal time.

Acknowledgements

We would like to appreciate @nkanada making recommendation of us to develop this site initially. We would like to express my gratitude to #99japan members. Advice and comments given by Yurie Makihara has been a great help in English proofreading for this paper. (This paper is written on the basis of (Aida *et al.*, 2013).)

References

Shin Aida, Yasutaka Shindo, and Masao Utiyama. 2011. *The automatically listing site extracted similar rescue requests*. http://www.selab.cs.tut.ac.jp/~aida/

Shin Aida, Yasutaka Shindo, and Masao Utiyama. 2013. *Rescue Activity for the Great East Japan Earthquake Based on a Website that Extracts Rescue Requests from the Net. Journal of Natural Language Processing*, 20(3):405–422.

Google. 2011. *More resources for those affected by the Japan earthquake and tsunami. The Official google.org blog*. http://blog.google.org/2011/03/more-resources-for-those-affected-by.html

Hiroaki Kuze. 2010. http://xtter.openlaszlo-ason.com/XTTER/1500ttr/

Koji Murakami *et al.* 2011. *ANPI NLP*. http://trans-aid.jp/ANPI_NLP/

Graham Neubig, Yuichiroh Matsubayashi, Masato Hagiwara, and Koji Murakami. 2011. *Safety Information Mining — What can NLP do in a disaster —. Proceedings of the 5th International Joint Conference on Natural Language Processing (IJCNLP)*, 965–973.

Haruyuki Seki *et al.* 2011. *sinsai.info*. http://www.sinsai.info/

Kaichi Tamiya. 2011. Tamiya's Blog: 東北関東大震災，救助依頼連絡先 *("Rescue Request Contact for The Great East Japan Earthquake")*. http://ameblo.jp/ktamiya/entry-10829792004.html

Kaichi Tamiya. 2011. 東北関東大震災の救助支援プロジェクト「#99japan」参加者を募集します *("We Invite the Participants of the Rescue Assistance Project #99japan in the The Great East Japan Earthquake")*. http://twipla.jp/events/6133

Fumi Yamazaki *et al.*. 2012. #shinsaidata「東日本大震災ビッグデータワークショップ — Project 311 —」ブレスト *("The Big Data Workshop of The Great East Japan Earthquake — Project 311 —: A Brainstorming on Twitter")*. http://togetter.com/li/372103

2channel users. 2011. 【私にも】三陸沖地震災害の情報支援【できる】*("Information support of The Great East Japan Earthquake Disaster")*. http://logsoku.com/thread/hayabusa.2ch.net/eq/1299829654/

2channel ID:nx64KwTT user. 2011. 東北大震災 まとめ *Wiki("The Great East Japan Earthquake Summary Wiki")*. http://www45.atwiki.jp/acuser001

#99japan. 2011. 共同編集: 被害リアルマップ東北地方太平洋沖地震 *("Rescue Request Map for the Great East Japan Earthquake Based on Google Maps")*. https://maps.google.co.jp/maps/ms?ie=UTF8&hl=ja&msa=0&ll=38.255436,140.998535&spn=10.259815,16.54541&z=6&msid=212756209350684899471.00049f93fb04a48b1dce9

#99japan. 2011. 共同編集: 物資 要請・提供マップ東北関東大震災 *("Supply Request Map for the Great East Japan Earthquake Based on Google Maps")*. https://maps.google.co.jp/maps/ms?ie=UTF8&hl=ja&msa=0&msid=212756209350684899471.00049ea27cf60c4292136&ll=37.827141,140.306396&spn=2.290855,3.488159

@ma_chiman. 2011. 東日本震災支援 #99japan（救急ジャパン）公式サイト *("Rescue Assistance Project for The Great East Japan Earthquake #99japan: Official Site")*. https://sites.google.com/site/sharp99japan/

A Framework and Tool for Collaborative Extraction of Reliable Information

Graham Neubig[1], **Shinsuke Mori**[2], **Masahiro Mizukami**[1]
[1]Graduate School of Information Science, Nara Institute of Science and Technology
8916-5 Takayama-cho, Ikoma-shi, Nara, Japan
[2]Academic Center for Computing and Media Studies, Kyoto University
Yoshida Honmachi, Sakyo-ku, Kyoto, Japan

Abstract

This research proposes a framework for efficient information extraction and filtering in situations where 1) extreme reliability is important, 2) the amount of information to be combed through is massive, and 3) we can expect a relatively large number of human workers to be available. In particular, we are motivated by needs in times of crisis, and assume that in order to ensure the high level of reliability required, it will be necessary to have at least one human worker confirm all extracted information. Given this setting, we propose a method to improve the efficiency of manual verification by deciding which information to present to workers using machine learning techniques. Even given this efficient search framework, the amount of information on the internet is still too much for one user to handle, so we additionally create a web-based framework that allows for collaborative work, and an algorithm that allows for this framework to work on large data in real-time. We perform an evaluation using data from Twitter after the Great East Japan Earthquake, and compare efficiency using both traditional keyword search and the proposed learning-based method.

1 Introduction

In times of crisis, internet sites, and particularly social networks such as Twitter,[1] overflow with information, with some reports noting an increase of activity by as much as 20 fold (Miyabe et al., 2012a). This information spans all genres, from questions or comments about the state of affairs, statements of opinion, emotional pleas, or even the spread of false rumors (Qu et al., 2009; Mendoza et al., 2010). Perhaps the information of the most interest is that which helps either crisis-responders or evacuees get a better grasp of situation (Vieweg et al., 2010), and this is particularly true when the information is provided directly by people in the disaster-affected areas (Starbird et al., 2012).

However, distinguishing useful information (e.g. "there is water at the evacuation center in Sendai high school") from unreliable or non-actionable information (e.g. "just arrived at the evacuation center, so tired...") takes a large amount of human effort. Luckily, however, the effort of good-willed internet users is one thing that is often plentiful in times of crisis. There have been many success stories where volunteers have banded together to turn natural language data into machine-readable format (Starbird and Stamberger, 2010), translate crisis-related information (Munro, 2010), gather survivor lists from evacuation sites and enter them into a central database (Google Japan, 2011), or even annotate data for the creation of specialized information extraction systems (Neubig et al., 2011). Given the large amount of work required in these *collaborative* efforts, it is common for as many as hundreds of volunteers to be involved in any single task.

On the other hand, examinations of the types of information provided on social networks after crises have shown that the number of possible information extraction tasks is large (20-30 by Corvey et al. (2012)'s classification). Information requirements also vary greatly from situation to situation, with the direction of the wind being important during the Oklahoma wildfires, and radiation measurements being important after the nuclear meltdown following the Great East Japan Earthquake (Vieweg et al., 2010; Doan et al., 2012). While a large number of volunteers may be mobilized for a single task, scaling this approach to tens or hundreds of disparate tasks has not proven

[1]`http://twitter.com/` retrieved on 2013-4-9.

possible given in a timely fashion. However, by increasing the *efficiency* of each volunteer, it is possible to reduce the overall number of volunteers needed, thus increasing the potential to tackle a much larger number of tasks in the short timeframe allowed after a disaster.

As a result, there have been a number of works that attempt to remove the requirement for manual labor by automating the information extraction process. For example, it has been noted that it may be possible to automatically identify information that contributes to situational awareness in general (Verma et al., 2011), or for more pinpoint tasks such as identifying information about safety of evacuees (Neubig et al., 2011), evacuation routes (Ishino et al., 2012), or information providers in disaster affected areas (Starbird et al., 2012). While these systems are quite promising, taking human workers out of the loop completely raises questions regarding the *reliability* of the information provided.

Given this background, in this work we examine a framework that enables teams of volunteers to identify useful information in a fashion that is *efficient*, *collaborative*, and highly *reliable*. In particular, to ensure reliability, we assume that all information provided must be checked by at least one volunteer. However, we increase the efficiency of this manual verification by learning a classifier to decide which pieces of information are likely to be relevant and should be presented to volunteers. Each time a new piece of information is labeled as either relevant or irrelevant to the task at hand, the classifier is updated to be more accurate at the task. Finally, to take advantage of collaborative work, we implement the proposed framework in a web interface that can be used collaboratively by many workers simultaneously.

Overall, while each of the individual components described below are not novel (quite standard, in fact), our work makes four major contributions: 1) combining these techniques into one over-spanning framework for efficient information extraction (Section 2), 2) proposal and evaluation of the information extraction framework in a collaborative setting, something that has not covered extensively in previous work (Section 3), 3) a relatively extensive manual evaluation of the framework on real large-scale data in times of crisis (Section 4), and 4) an open-source implementation of the proposed framework.[2]

2 Information Filtering/Extraction Framework

As mentioned in the previous section, the overall goal of this paper is to efficiently extract reliable information from the internet. To formalize this notion, we define the target of the information extraction system as a collection of documents $\mathcal{D} = \{D_1, \ldots, D_I\}$. From a given document D_i we would like to gather all pieces of information $T_i = \{\boldsymbol{t}_{i,1}, \ldots, \boldsymbol{t}_{i,J}\}$ relevant to our given task. Each piece of information is vector containing K slots to be filled $\boldsymbol{t}_{i,j} = \{t_{i,j,1}, \ldots, t_{i,j,K}\}$. In addition, we define $\mathcal{U} = \{u_1, \ldots, u_I\}$ where each u_i corresponds to document D_i and indicates whether there is at least one piece of useful information in the document $u_i := (|T_i| > 0)$.

To give a concrete example, let us assume that the information we are interested in is evacuation areas after a crisis, and the target that we are extracting from is Twitter posts. In this case, each document D_i would be a Twitter post, and u_i would be a binary variable indicating whether there is any useful information in the post. $\boldsymbol{t}_{i,j}$ would be a set of entries about a particular evacuation site, where each column may indicate traits of the evacuation site such as "city," "address," and "current status."

In the following two sections, we describe the proposed framework for finding this information in two steps: *filtering*, where we estimate the usefulness u_i of each document, and *extraction*, where we extract the information T_i from documents that pass the filtering process. In particular we focus on filtering useful documents from a large document collection, and use a simple manual extraction process.

2.1 Information Filtering

We first describe two approaches to information filtering: a baseline of keyword search, and our improved method based on relevance feedback.

2.1.1 Keyword Search

Almost any attempt to find information in a large document collection will start with keyword search, where documents are retrieved according to a user query Q. In the terminology that we introduced above, this means that u_i will be true ei-

[2] Available at `http://phontron.com/webigator`

ther when all of the keywords match

$$u_i := (|D_i \cap Q| = |Q|) \quad (1)$$

or when at least one of the keywords matches

$$u_i := (|D_i \cap Q| > 0). \quad (2)$$

While this technique is extremely simple, it has also proven useful in actual rescue efforts that monitor social networks for information in times of crisis (Aida et al., 2012).

2.1.2 Information Filtering using Classifiers

However, keyword search is clearly not sophisticated enough to adequately make the decision whether a particular document contains information useful to a particular task, with the "and" search in Equation (1) filtering out too many documents, and the "or" search in Equation (2) picking up too much noise. As a solution to this problem, it is common to use machine learning to create more sophisticated classifiers (Sebastiani, 2002).

Here, we overview classifiers in the case of binary classification between $u_i = 1$ (true) and $u_i = 0$ (false). In this case, we define N feature functions $\phi_n(D_i)$ that express various characteristics of the document D_i. Each feature function is assigned a weight λ_n and the weighted sum of feature functions is the document's score $s(D_i)$

$$s(D_i) = \sum_{n=1}^{N} \lambda_n \phi_n(D_i). \quad (3)$$

In the case of $s(D_i) \geq 0$, D_i is classified as a positive example, and in the case of $s(D_i) < 0$, D_i is classified as a negative example.

In order to learn the weights $\boldsymbol{\lambda} = (\lambda_1, \lambda_2, \ldots, \lambda_K)$, a corpus of documents $\mathcal{D}$ is annotated with labels $\mathcal{U}^*$, and a classifier such as support vector machines (SVMs) or naive Bayes classifiers is used to train the weight values (Joachims, 1998). In this research, we use naive Bayes classifiers as they are extremely fast to learn and perform reasonably well on document classification tasks (Dumais et al., 1998). In naive Bayes classifiers, we calculate the conditional probability of label u given the feature ϕ_n

$$P(u = 1|\phi_n) = c(\phi_n, u^* = 1)/c(\phi_n)$$

where we slightly abuse notation for clarity by defining $c(\phi_n)$ to be the sum of all values of $\phi_n(D_i)$ for labeled documents and $c(\phi_n, u^* = 1)$ to be the same sum for documents labeled with $u^* = 1$. The probability of a label given the document is the product of the feature probabilities

$$P(u_i = 1|D_i) = \prod_n P(u = 1|\phi_n)^{\phi_n(D_i)}/Z$$

where Z is normalizes the probabilities to add to 1

$$Z = P(u_i = 1|D_i) + P(u_i = 0|D_i).$$

We can define score $s(D_i)$ as the log odds of $P(u_i = 1|D_i)$

$$s(D_i) = \log P(u_i = 1|D_i) - \log P(u_i = 0|D_i)$$

which allows us to define each weight λ_n as

$$\lambda_n = \log c(\phi_n, u^* = 1) - \log c(\phi_n, u^* = 0).$$

However, zero counts for either positive or negative labels will cause the log odds to be negative or positive infinity, so in many cases, the counts are augmented with a pseudo-count α for smoothing (Mackay and Petoy, 1995):

$$\lambda_n = \log(c(\phi_n, u^* = 1) + \alpha) - \log(c(\phi_n, u^* = 0) + \alpha). \quad (4)$$

It should also be noted that while standard classifiers are trained using the document labels $\mathcal{U}$, it is also possible to directly label the features ϕ_n (Melville et al., 2009; Settles, 2011). In this case, let $l(\phi_n, u^* = 1)$ be a function that is 1 if feature ϕ_n is labeled positive, and 0 otherwise. We further augment Equation (4) with a pseudo-count β in the case of labeled features

$$\lambda_n = \log(c(\phi_n, u^* = 1) + \alpha + \beta l(\phi_n, u^* = 1)) - \log(c(\phi_n, u^* = 0) + \alpha + \beta l(\phi_n, u^* = 0)). \quad (5)$$

In other words, if a positively labeled feature exists in a particular document D_i, that document will have a higher chance of being labeled positive. This is useful in our situation, as any classifier we build will likely be combined with keyword search as described in the previous section, and the features corresponding to these keywords can automatically be labeled as positive.

The bottleneck in the construction of these classifiers is the manual creation of the labels $\mathcal{U}^*$, which takes a significant amount of time and effort. Fortunately, there has been some movement for disaster preparation to create labeled corpora in the crisis-related domain (Verma et al., 2011; Neubig et al., 2011; Corvey et al., 2012). However, as all pre-constructed resources, these will be necessarily limited to tasks forseen before an actual disaster occurs, and also limited by the language of the resources (i.e. English or Japanese).

2.1.3 On-the-fly Information Filtering with Relevance Feedback

In the framework in this paper, we propose using a different approach that requires no prior creation of labels $\mathcal{U}^*$ (and thus no foresight into the information that may be necessary in any particular situation), but also can take advantage of machine learning techniques to improve the accuracy of information filtering. In order to do so, we start with no labels and simple keyword search, but utilize the framework of *relevance feedback* (Zhou and Huang, 2003) to iteratively improve the classifier. The iterative process is as follows:

Search: From all unlabeled documents in $\mathcal{D}$ with at least one matching keyword, the system selects M documents with the highest score $s(D_i)$ and displays them to the user.

Extraction/Feedback: The user extracts information T_i from each document D_i (as described in the following section), and notes through the interface whether the document had any useful information ($u_i^* = 1$) or did not ($u_i^* = 0$).

Learning: Once the user finishes extracting information from the M documents, the new labels are submitted to the learning algorithm, weights are updated, and we return to step 1.

This process is extremely simple, but also satisfies a number of desiderata for our system. First, before any examples are labeled, it is possible to use simple keyword search as a starting point, so users can start search immediately without any prior labeling of data.[3] However, we still have the potential to greatly improve efficiency by learning a classifier that can reduce the number of false examples ($u_i^* = 0$) that the user has to view. Second, the labeling criterion is extremely intuitive: if useful information that can be added to the database is found, the label is positive, and if useful information is not found the label is negative. Thus, users can essentially perform search exactly as they would normally, but the accuracy of the search results improves after each set of M documents is viewed and labeled.

[3]It is also theoretically possible, and likely useful to update the keywords during the annotation process. This is supported by the interface, but we decided to avoid keyword updating in our experiments to reduce the number of factors influencing results.

2.2 Information Extraction

The final part of the framework is the process of extracting information T_i from each document D_i. This is an interesting problem in its own right, with large amounts of work on automated methods (Sarawagi, 2008). There are also some works on the extraction of highly reliable information by including a human in the extraction practice by either writing regular expressions (Caruana et al., 2000), or by correcting mistakes made by automatic extraction methods (Kristjansson et al., 2004; Culotta and McCallum, 2005). While these works are relevant to our current task, our evaluation experiments are run on very short documents, for which the relevant information can manually be read, copied, and pasted into a spreadsheet with relatively high speed. Thus, in this work, the extraction of information from relevant documents is performed entirely by hand, and we leave expansion to more sophisticated methods to future work.

3 Collaborative Interface

While the method described in the previous section allows for efficient and reliable information filtering for a single worker over small-scale data, it cannot be trivially applied to larger data. The reason for this is two-fold. First, to implement the method described in the previous section, every example must be re-scored every time the classifier weights change, which results in a wait time between each example that linearly increases with the size of data at hand. Second, the previously described method assumes that there is only a single worker, but there are physical limits on the amount of data that a single worker can handle.

In this section, we further improve the framework presented in the previous section by implementing it as a streaming and collaborative information aggregation interface. The framework handles information streams by not re-scoring every possibly example, but performing greedy re-

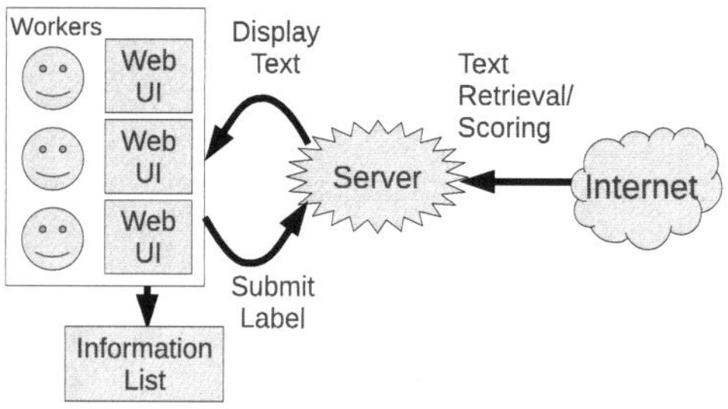

Figure 1: Overview of the proposed framework

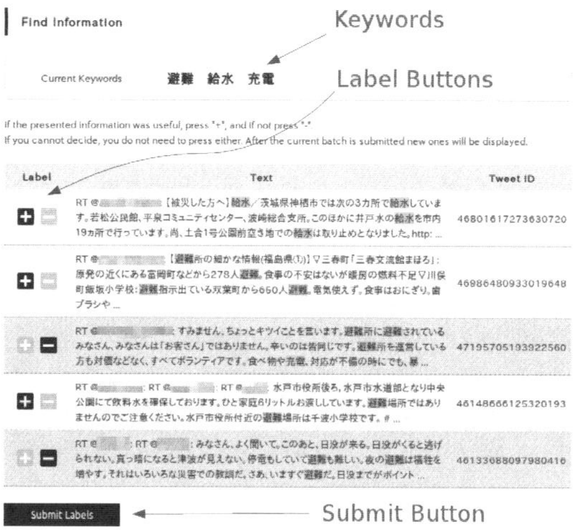

Figure 2: Example of the annotation interface

scoring of only candidates to be presented to workers and keeping a limited number of top-scoring candidates in a memory cache. The framework is collaborative as it is implemented through a multi-user web interface that communicates with the scoring and aggregation server running in the background. An overview of the framework is shown in Figure 1.

We also show an example of the annotation interface in Figure 2. On the task page, there is a place to view and enter the keywords for the current task, and several (in this case, five) examples to be viewed and labeled by the worker. Once the worker has viewed all instances, and clicked either "+" for positive or "-" for negative, the labels can be submitted to the server to update the weights.

3.1 Work Flow from the User Side

We assume a use case where we have a small group of users, and one of the users is designated as the leader of the group.

Before the users commence the information filtering process, the group decides the type of information they want to extract (e.g. "information about evacuation areas within Miyagi prefecture"). Next, the users choose one or more keywords related to this information (e.g. "miyagi", "evacuation"). The group leader then creates a location where all of the users can aggregate information to the specified topic using an online document management service such as Google Docs,[4] or a special-purpose web site. Every user in the group then accesses the annotation interface, labels instances, and inputs the useful information found in positive instances into the location where the information is being aggregated. To ensure that multiple users are not viewing the same information, each document is only displayed to a single user.

3.2 Work Flow from the Server Side

When the group leader specifies the first keywords to be used in the task, the computation server starts to acquire examples from a web information source such as Twitter. There is a certain amount of overhead required to run even a simple classifier such as that described in Section 2.1.2, so to increase the efficiency of information retrieval we first perform a simple keyword filtering step that removes all documents that do not contain at least one instance of one of the specified keywords.

Given the keyword-filtered document stream, the server then calculates the features and current scores for each of the incoming documents. These documents are inserted into a cache ordered in descending order of score. In cases where it is necessary to save memory, the cache size can be limited appropriately, with low scoring candidates being omitted from the cache and permanently removed from consideration.

Similarly to the previous section, when the user labels an example, this label is fed back to the system and weights are retrained appropriately. However, re-scoring every document in the cache each time the weights are updated will result in a large time lag at each update. In order to reduce this lag, we propose a method for approximately discovering the highest scoring example in the cache without re-scoring every example.

Specifically, we would like to display high-scoring examples to the user, but unless we recalculate scores for the entire cache on every model update there is a possibility that some of

[4] `http://docs.google.com` retrieved on 2013-4-9.

the scores in the cache will be calculated by an older version of the model. In order to solve this problem in an efficient manner, we note that even though the scores may change somewhat, in most cases the order of the scores will remain more-or-less the same as it was before the update. We further take advantage of this by greedily searching for the highest scoring example according to the following process:

1. According to the (potentially old) scores in the cache, find the highest scoring example d_1 and second-highest scoring example d_2.
2. Re-calculate d_1's score according to the current version of the model.
3. Compare the score of d_1 to the score of the example d_2 according to the *old* model.[5]
4. If d_1's new score is higher than d_2's old score, return d_1 as the highest-scoring example. Otherwise, re-insert d_1 into the cache and return to step 1.

It should be noted that this search is greedy, and thus may make mistakes when d_1's score is larger than d_2, but not larger than examples that occur farther down in the cache.

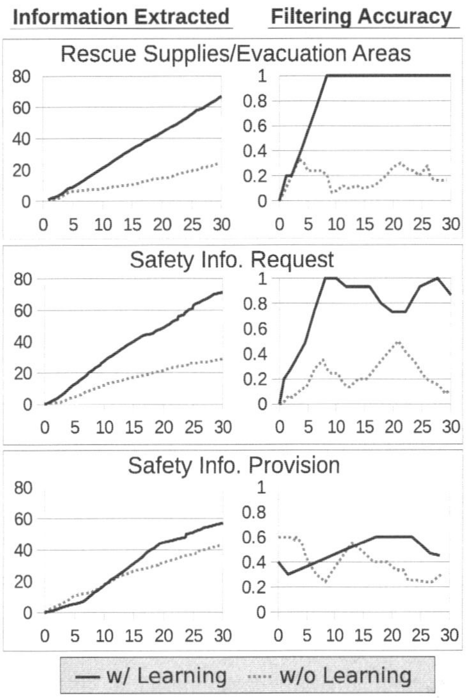

Figure 3: Results for three tasks with regards to pieces of information extracted and the 5-minute rolling average percentage of presented tweets that contained useful information. The horizontal axis is time in minutes.

4 Experimental Evaluation

To evaluate the effectiveness of our proposed framework and tool for extraction of highly reliable information, we perform a series of experimental evaluations. As extraction of highly reliable information is particularly important in times of crisis, we used data provided as part of the Great East Japan Earthquake Big Data Workshop[6] including all actual Japanese tweets from Twitter for one week after the earthquake starting at March 11th, 2011, 14:45, a total of 179 million tweets.

We specify three information extraction tasks as shown in Table 1, and use these as the targets for our experiments. The first task consists of finding information about evacuation areas or rescue supplies that may be useful to those in disaster-affected areas, and the other two tasks are related to finding posts either requesting or providing information about the safety of evacuees.

Given our goal of efficient and reliable identification and extraction of information as stated in Section 1, we use as our evaluation measure the number of tweets able to be verified by workers in 30 minutes. In addition, to more closely simulate the actual situation of the tool being used in a crisis-response setting, all workers were asked to fill in a web form indicating information such as "location," "situation," or "name" in accordance to the information that would likely be useful for each of the tasks.

Given this data and these tasks, we perform two rounds of experiments to compare the efficiency of the learning-based interface compared to simple keyword search (Section 4.1) and the efficacy of collaborative work (Section 4.2).

[5]We use d_2's old model score because the cache order will change the most when the user labels an example as negative. In these cases, if both d_1 and d_2 are similar to the negatively labeled example, both will see a large reduction in score, so we d_1's new score will be much smaller than d_2's old score, but not necessarily smaller than d_2's new score. To ensure that we continue penalizing high-scoring instances that are similar to the negatively labeled instance, we continue updating the cache until we find an example that both had a high score according to the old model (and thus a high position in the cache), and a high score according to the new model.

[6]`https://sites.google.com/site/prj311/`

Type	Keywords
Evacuation/Rescue Supplies	避難所 (evacuation area), 給水 (water supplies), 炊き出し (food supplies)
Safety Info. Request	連絡 (contact), 取れない (cannot), 待って (waiting)
Safety Info. Provision	連絡 (contact), 無事 (safe)

Table 1: Filtered information and corresponding keywords

4.1 Evaluation of Learning-based Information Filtering

First, we perform an evaluation of the information filtering interface described in Section 2.1.3. As features, we use character 1-to-5-grams,[7] and a naive Bayes classifier, as it is extremely efficient to both classify and update. In Equation (5), we set $\alpha = 1$ and $\beta = 5$. As a baseline system, we use simple keyword search. All results were provided by a single user who had time to practice using the interface before results were recorded.

We show the results for the three tasks in Figure 3. From the results indicating the number of pieces of useful information extracted on the left side of the graph, we can see that the proposed learning capability improves the efficiency, with increases ranging from 35%-159%. This increase can be largely attributed to an increase in the information filtering accuracy, or the number of documents displayed to the user that have at least one piece of useful information. The rolling average of accuracy is shown on the right side of Figure 3.

We can see that there is a significant difference in the information filtering accuracy between tasks, and this affects the gain afforded by the learning capability. Specifically, "Safety Info. Provision" has lower accuracy than the other tasks, largely because it is difficult to distinguish between provision of information ("I heard that XXX is safe") and requests for information ("I wonder if XXX is safe"), while the latter is much more common in the corpus (approximately five times according to Murakami and Hagiwara (2012)'s estimate). Thus, for more difficult tasks improving the accuracy of the classifiers could lead to further improvements in the gains provided by the proposed technique.

4.2 Evaluation of the Collaborative Interface

In addition, to evaluate the collaborative web interface described in Section 3, we performed experiments in which multiple annotators worked collaboratively on an information filtering task. The experimental setup is identical to that described in the previous section, but we focus only on the Evacuation/Rescue Supplies task. As a comparison, we compare results for when 1, 2, or 3 users work collaboratively on a single information filtering task, performing two experiments for each number of users.

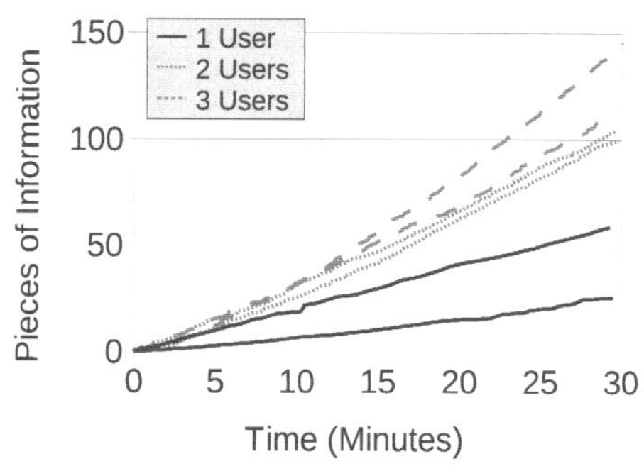

Figure 4: Information verified by 1, 2, or 3 users

The result of this experiment is shown in Figure 4. After 30 minutes of work, a single user had extracted an average of 43 pieces, two users had extracted 103 pieces, and three users had extracted 129 pieces of useful information and added them to the shared aggregation site. Thus, we can see that increasing the number of users results in an approximately linear increase in the amount of information extracted, confirming the effectiveness of allowing multiple users to work on a single task, and share the results of labeling with a single classifier. As each worker works largely independently, we hypothesize that this trend will continue for even larger numbers of users.

In Figure 5 we show the improvement in efficiency of information extraction as each run progresses. From the graph, we can see that in all cases, the efficiency at the end of the run has increased by 1.3-2.0 times over that achieved in the initial five minutes. Figure 6 displays the rolling average of positive examples, and we can see that

[7]Character n-grams remove the effect of analysis mistakes that occur when performing Japanese tokenization on non-standard text such Twitter.

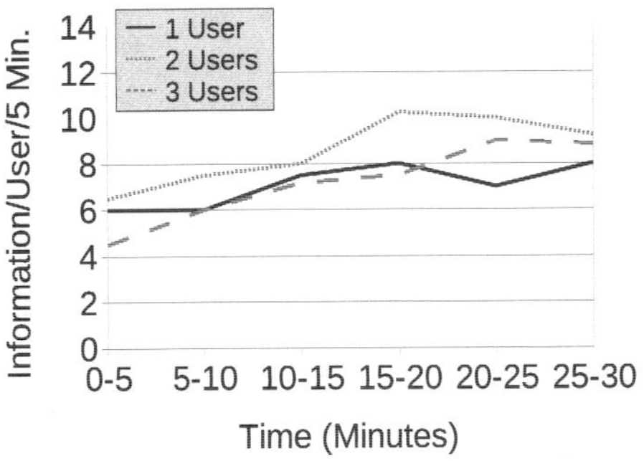

Figure 5: Average pieces of information added by one user in each time frame

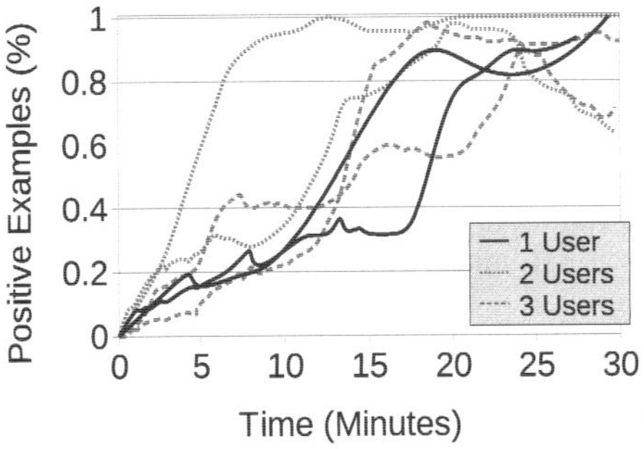

Figure 6: The percentage of examples labeled as positive in each trial run

the percentage of positive examples labeled increases drastically over time, with accuracy near 100% achieved in four out of six trials, and all trials achieving accuracy over 60%. However, compared to this large increase in the accuracy of the examples presented to users, the increase in the amount of information extracted is small. This is because even after positive information has been identified, there is a small but fixed amount of work required to enter the useful information into the information aggregation site. As a result, we can expect that further improvements in information extraction efficiency can be achieved by automatically extracting candidates to fill in each column of information to be extracted, and make it possible for a human to simply press a button to verify the information if it happens to be correct.

5 Conclusion/Future Work

In this paper, we presented a framework to efficiently, reliably, and collaboratively filter and extract useful information from the large and noisy web, with a focus of information extraction from Twitter during crisis situations. As a result, we found that the proposed framework led to an increase in efficiency of 35%-159% over simple keyword search, with further gains possible when more than one user participates in the information extraction process.

As future work, we can think of expansions to multi-class information extraction problems. In this paper, we limited our experiments to situations where each classifier is trained to identify a single type of information, so identifying three types of information will require three separate rounds of classifier training. While this is a simple setup for users to understand, it is inefficient in the case of a large number of classes, so it is worth examining the possibilities of extracting multiple types of information in a single process.

Another interesting line of work is the provision of extracted information in an easy-to-consume form for people in disaster areas through a QA system that can be accessed through telephone when other communication tools such as the internet are not available (Kazama et al., 2012).

Assessing the reliability of information on the web is an important challenge, particularly in times of crisis (Mendoza et al., 2010). Work to automatically assess the reliability of information may focus on classifiers assessing the text, user, topic, and dispersal patterns of the said information (Castillo et al., 2011) or comments on social networks casting doubt on said information's veracity (Miyabe et al., 2012b). These methods could be combined with our information extraction method to further ensure the reliability of the extracted information.

There are also a number of improvements that could be made to the extraction algorithm itself. For example, while in this work we used a simple Naive Bayes classifier, there are classifiers developed specifically for the task of classifying positive examples (Schölkopf et al., 2001), which may increase the accuracy of information identification. Other promising directions include the application of more advanced information extraction techniques, the identification of information that is identical to information that has already been extracted, or application to crowd-sourcing platforms such as Mechanical Turk.

Acknowledgments

The authors sincerely thank Shingo Murakami for his assistance in developing the web interface during the Great East Japan Earthquake Big Data Workshop. We would also like to thank all of the subjects who lent their time to participate in manual annotation experiments, and the oranizers of the Great East Japan Earthquake Big Data Workshop and Twitter for providing the data that made the experiments possible.

References

Shin Aida, Yasutaka Shindoh, and Masao Utiyama. 2012. Regarding the creation of the "Great East Japan Earthquake rescue request information extraction site" and rescue activities (in Japanese). In *Proc. 18th NLP*.

Rich Caruana, Paul G. Hodor, and John Rosenberg. 2000. High precision information extraction. In *Proc. of the KDD-2000 Workshop on Text Mining*.

Carlos Castillo, Marcelo Mendoza, and Barbara Poblete. 2011. Information credibility on Twitter. In *Proc. WWW*, pages 675–684.

William J Corvey, Sudha Verma, Sarah Vieweg, Martha Palmer, and James H Martin. 2012. Foundations of a multilayer annotation framework for Twitter communications during crisis events. In *Proc. LREC*, pages 21–27.

Aron Culotta and Andrew McCallum. 2005. Reducing labeling effort for structured prediction tasks. In *Proc. AAAI*.

Son Doan, Bao-Khanh Ho Vo, and Nigel Collier. 2012. An analysis of Twitter messages in the 2011 Tohoku earthquake. In *Electronic Healthcare*, pages 58–66.

Susan Dumais, John Platt, David Heckerman, and Mehran Sahami. 1998. Inductive learning algorithms and representations for text categorization. In *Proc. CIKM*, pages 148–155.

Google Japan. 2011. Requesting your help to register shared survivor lists to Person Finder (in Japanese). `http://googlejapan.blogspot.com/2011/03/blog-post_17.html`.

Aya Ishino, Shuhei Odawara, Hidetsugu Nanba, and Toshiyuki Takezawa. 2012. Extracting transportation information and traffic problems from tweets during a disaster. In *Proc. IMMM*, pages 91–96.

Thorsten Joachims. 1998. Text categorization with support vector machines: Learning with many relevant features. In *ECML-98*.

Jun'ichi Kazama, Stijn De Saeger, Kentaro Torisawa, Jun Goto, and Istvan Varga. 2012. An attempt to apply a QA system to information in times of crisis (in Japanese). In *Proc. 18th NLP*.

Trausti Kristjansson, Aron Culotta, Paul Viola, and Andrew McCallum. 2004. Interactive information extraction with constrained conditional random fields. In *Proc. AAAI*.

David J.C. Mackay and Linda C. Bauman Petoy. 1995. A hierarchical Dirichlet language model. *Natural Language Engineering*, 1.

Prem Melville, Wojciech Gryc, and Richard D. Lawrence. 2009. Sentiment analysis of blogs by combining lexical knowledge with text classification. In *Proc. KDD*.

Marcelo Mendoza, Barbara Poblete, and Carlos Castillo. 2010. Twitter under crisis: can we trust what we RT? In *Proceedings of the First Workshop on Social Media Analytics (SOMA)*, pages 71–79.

Mai Miyabe, Asako Miura, and Eiji Aramaki. 2012a. Use trend analysis of Twitter after the Great East Japan Earthquake. In *Proc. CSCW*, pages 175–178.

Mai Miyabe, Ayana Umeshima, Akiyo Nadamoto, and Eiji Aramaki. 2012b. Rumor cloud: Gathering rumors by extracting correction information mentioned by humans (in Japanese). In *Proc. 18th NLP*.

Robert Munro. 2010. Crowdsourced translation for emergency response in Haiti: the global collaboration of local knowledge. In *Proc. AMTA Workshop on Collaborative Crowdsourcing for Translation*.

Koji Murakami and Masato Hagiwara. 2012. A detailed analysis of a safety information Tweet corpus and observations about its annotation (in Japanese). In *Proc. 18th NLP*.

Graham Neubig, Yuichiroh Matsubayashi, Masato Hagiwara, and Koji Murakami. 2011. Safety information mining - what can NLP do in a disaster -. In *Proc. IJCNLP*, pages 965–973, Chiang Mai, Thailand, November.

Yan Qu, Philip Fei Wu, and Xiaoqing Wang. 2009. Online community response to major disaster: A study of Tianya forum in the 2008 Sichuan earthquake. In *Proc. HICSS*, pages 1–11. IEEE.

Sunita Sarawagi. 2008. Information extraction. *Foundations and trends in databases*, 1(3):261–377.

Bernhard Schölkopf, John C. Platt, John Shawe-Taylor, Alex J. Smola, and Robert C. Williamson. 2001. Estimating the support of a high-dimensional distribution. *Neural computation*, 13(7):1443–1471.

Fabrizio Sebastiani. 2002. Machine learning in automated text categorization. *ACM Comput. Surv.*, 34(1).

Burr Settles. 2011. Closing the loop: Fast, interactive semi-supervised annotation with queries on features and instances. In *Proc. EMNLP*.

Kate Starbird and Jeannie Stamberger. 2010. Tweak the tweet: Leveraging microblogging proliferation with a prescriptive syntax to support citizen reporting. In *Proc. ISCRAM*.

Kate Starbird, Grace Muzny, and Leysia Palen. 2012. Learning from the crowd: Collaborative filtering techniques for identifying on-the-ground Twitterers during mass disruptions. In *Proc. ISCRAM*.

Sudha Verma, Sarah Vieweg, William J Corvey, Leysia Palen, James H Martin, Martha Palmer, Aaron Schram, and Kenneth M Anderson. 2011. Natural language processing to the rescue?: Extracting'situational awareness' tweets during mass emergency. *Proc. ICWSM*.

Sarah Vieweg, Amanda L Hughes, Kate Starbird, and Leysia Palen. 2010. Microblogging during two natural hazards events: what Twitter may contribute to situational awareness. In *Proc. CHI*, pages 1079–1088.

Xiang Sean Zhou and Thomas S. Huang. 2003. Relevance feedback in image retrieval: A comprehensive review. *Multimedia systems*, 8(6).

Extracting and Aggregating False Information from Microblogs

Naoaki Okazaki[†‡] Keita Nabeshima[†] Kento Watanabe[†]

Junta Mizuno[§] Kentaro Inui[†]

{okazaki, nabeshima, kento.w, junta-m, inui}@ecei.tohoku.ac.jp

[†]Graduate School of Information Sciences, Tohoku University
6-3-09 Aramakiaza-Aoba, Aoba-ku, Sendai, 980-8579 Japan

[‡]Precursory Research for Embryonic Science and Technology (PREST), Japan Science and Technology Agency (JST)

[§]National Institute of Information and Communications Technology (NICT)

Abstract

During the 2011 East Japan Earthquake and Tsunami Disaster, we had found a number of false information spread on Twitter, e.g., "The Cosmo Oil explosion causes toxic rain." This paper extracts pieces of false information exhaustively from all the tweets within one week after the earthquake. Designing a set of linguistic patterns that correct false information, this paper proposes a method for detecting false information. More specifically, the method extracts text passages that match to the correction patterns, clusters the passages into topics of false information, and selects, for each topic, a passage explaining the false information the most suitably. In the experiment, we report the performance of the proposed method on the data set extracted manually from Web sites that are specialized in collecting false information.

1 Introduction

In the aftermath of the Tohoku Earthquake (also known as the Great East Japan Earthquake) in March 2011, social media, such as the Twitter social networking and microblogging service, served as highly active and beneficial sources of information. Among Internet users, 18.3% referred to social media as information sources, 18.6% referred to Internet newspapers, and 23.1% referred to national and regional government websites (Nomura Research Institute, 2011). This indicates that social media rivaled the other two in influence. It has also been noted that the Internet and social media has accelerated the dissemination of disinformation and other types of misinformation, e.g., "Toxic rain will follow the explosion at the Cosmo Oil petrochemical complex".

Misinformation such as this regarding safety and danger spread quickly in the aftermath of the Tohoku Earthquake and the related accident at the Fukushima Dai-Ichi Nuclear Power Plant, which threatened the lives and welfare of numerous people. Other themes of the misinformation included the admonition, "Drink Isodine (povidone iodine) to protect your thyroid from radiation". One tweet consolidation site dedicated to collecting/correcting information on the Tohoku Earthquake[1] found that during the month of January 2012, even ten months after the event, more than ten pieces of misinformation related to the earthquake were posted. This indicates a strong need for misinformation alerts in normal times as well as in times of disaster.

In this study, we aim at automatic collection of misinformation disseminated on Twitter. More concretely, we focus on corrective patterns (CPs), such as *It is incorrect that ...*, which are commonly used to correct or refute misinformation, and propose a method incorporating such CPs into a system for automatic collection of misinformation. We then describe the experimental application of this method to tweets posted during the week following the Tohoku Earthquake. The results of this experiment showed that our method could detect approximately half of the 60 misinformative tweets identified by the existing misinformation consolidation sites, as well as 22 other misinformative tweets that had not been recorded on those sites.

2 Related work

Twitter has been the subject of a number of studies. Here, we review those relating to the truth or credibility of information posted on Twitter.

Qazvinian et al. (2011) proposed a method for classifying a group of tweets related to misinfor-

[1]https://twitter.com/#!/jishin_dema

mation (such as a group of tweets containing the terms "Barack Obama" and "Muslim") into those including explicit expression of misinformation (e.g., "Barack Obama is a Muslim"), and those that do not (e.g., "Barack Obama met with Muslim leaders"), then further classifying the latter into those that support the misinformation and those that oppose it. Unlike the present study, it assumed that mining misinformation from large volumes of tweet and obtaining a group of misinformation-related tweets was outside its scope.

In Japan, numerous studies have been performed on misinformation dissemination via Twitter, prompted by a strong awareness of this problem following the Tohoku Earthquake. For example, Fujikawa et al. (2012) proposed a method for assessing the truth or falsehood of information by classifying user reactions based on the number of specific responses, such as those expressing doubt or presenting well-grounded arguments that the topic is misinformative. Toriumi et al. (2012) proposed a method of investigating the co-occurrence of words and terms such as *disinformation*, *lie*, and *false report* in arguments related to tweet content in order to determine whether the content comprises misinformation.

To analyze the trends in misinformation dissemination and correction on Twitter following the Tohoku Earthquake, Umejima et al. (2011) tested hypotheses such as "the probability of tweet text containing a URL being misinformation is low", "many information tweets contain content that urges action, is negative, or fans unrest", and "a tweet containing any of these three features is apt to be retweeted". In subsequent studies (Umejima et al., 2012; Miyabe et al., 2012), their group showed that words and terms that clearly indicate an intention to correct, such as *disinformation* and *mistaken*, provide a useful feature for recognizing corrective tweets during the construction of a misinformation database. They collected tweets containing such terms and built a binary classifier to assess whether the tweets were correcting specific information.

In all of these studies, each tweet text is taken as a unit with the focus on determining whether it contains misinformation or corrects by providing specific information[2], without precisely identifying the region of the misinformation in the tweet text. Therefore, to our knowledge, the present study represents the first investigation of a comprehensive collection of misinformation extracted from large volumes of tweet data.

[2]For example, the tweet "Be careful! All kinds of misinformation are circulating on Twitter" contains the expression "misinformation" but does not correct any specific information.

3 Proposed method

In this study, we assume that misinformation disseminated on Twitter is corrected or refuted by other users. For example, we found tweets correcting information (*corrective tweets* hereafter) for the misinformation, "Toxic rain is falling because of the Cosmo Oil explosion."

- <u>It is counterfactual that</u> toxic rain will fall due to the Cosmo Oil explosion.
- Be aware of the <u>false rumors that</u> rain contaminated by the toxic substances produced by the Cosmo Oil explosion will fall.

A corrective tweet consists of a corrective expression (e.g., the underlined parts in the above examples) and misinformation where the corrective expression corrects or refutes. Thus, we can locate misinformation by finding corrective expressions in tweets. The goal of the proposed method presented in this section is to collect phrases of misinformation by using corrective patterns (CPs) and aggregate them into a small number of descriptions of misinformation.

Figure 1 shows the flow of the proposed method, which is essentially comprised of the four steps. In Step 1, the proposed method searches for occurrences of CPs in tweets and extracts their targets of correction (*corrected phrases* hereafter). Step 2 chooses keywords that appear frequently in the corrected phrases. In order to merge keywords referring to the same misinformation, we cluster keywords (Step 3). Finally in Step 4, the proposed method chooses the small number of phrases that describe misinformation the most suitably. We will explain the detail of these steps in the subsequent subsections.

3.1 Step 1: Extraction of corrected phrases

Here, we search for tweets with corrected phrases. In corrective tweets, the search determines the presence of the misinformation that is being corrected or refuted via terms such as *misinformation* or *mistaken*, as in the statement, "It is disinformation that <u>Isodine provides protection against radiation</u>", in

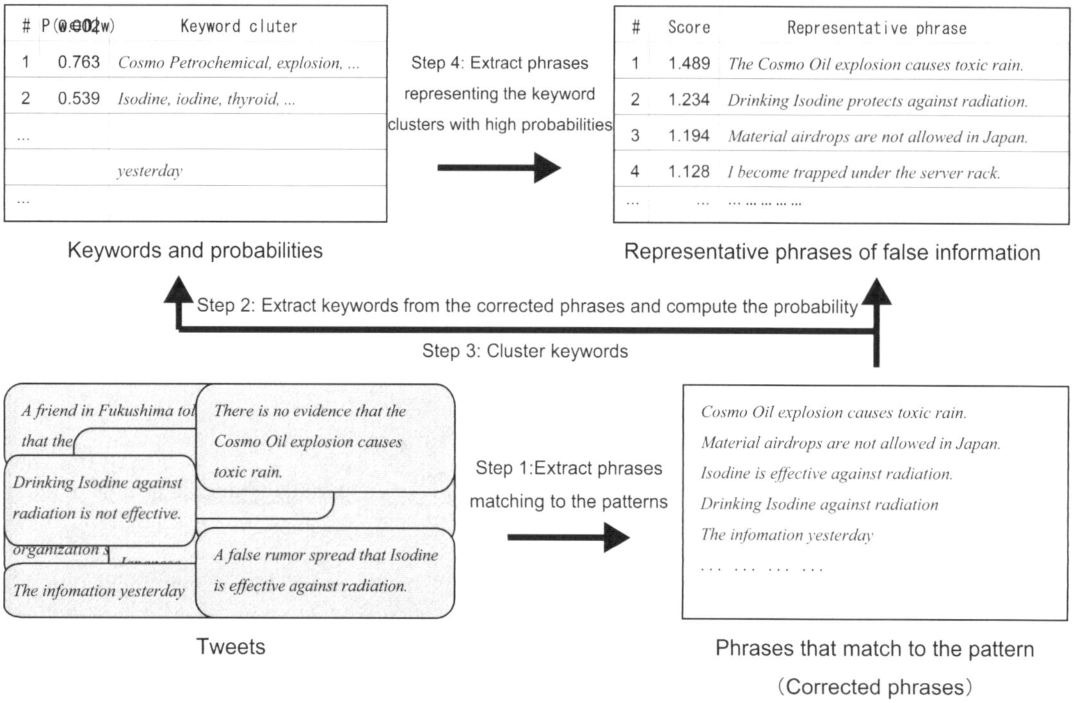

Figure 1: Overview of the proposed method

which the underlined portion is the misinformative phrase being corrected. A Japanese translation of this sentence is, "Isojin ha hibaku wo fusegeru to iu no wa dema da".

In the Japanese sentence that corrects or refutes misinformation, the corrected phrase (e.g., in transliteration, the underlined portion of the sentence "Isojin ha hibaku wo fusegeru", which corresponds to the underlined portion of the above English example) is followed by a functional attributive particle expression, such as the above "to iu no wa" or some other functionally similar term such as "no yo na", and the corrective expression ("wa dema da" in the above example).

We manually formulated 368 CPs to recognize the corrected phrases. We obtained these CPs by examining tweets containing keywords that correspond to 15 kinds of well-known misinformation. If a region of a tweet text matches any of these CPs, the corrected phrase is deemed to comprise the portion of the Japanese sentence ranging from the first word in the sentence to just before the CP. We applied this process to the whole of the tweets under investigation, and the set of corrected phrases extracted in this way is denoted as D.

3.2 Step 2: Keyword extraction

Some of the corrected phrases extracted in this way simply refer to the misinformation rather than stating it, as in "kino no are" (literally "That thing yesterday") in a sentence such as "kino no are wa dema da" ("That thing yesterday was misinformation"). Such phrases cannot be considered misinformative and must therefore be excluded. This is done by determining whether the words in the corrected phrase co-occur prominently with the CPs. For this purpose, the conditional probability that a word w used in the tweet is among those in the corrected phrase set D is computed as,

$$P(w \in D|w) = \frac{\text{\# tweets where } w \text{ co-occurs with CPs}}{\text{\# tweets containing } w}. \quad (1)$$

We extract the top-500 words yielding the highest probability as misinformation keywords.

3.3 Step 3: Keyword clustering

Misinformative phrases pertaining to the same information may differ considerably in wording and information quantity, as in "Rain containing hazardous substances from the Cosmo Oil fire will occur" and "The Cosmo Oil explosion is toxic", which must be consolidated to avoid redundancy when extracting misinformation. For this reason, we perform clustering of the keywords extracted in Step 2. As the inter-keyword distance (i.e., similarity), we use the cosine similarity on context vectors whose elements correspond to co-occurrence counts between the keywords and the content words (nouns, verbs, and adjectives) in sentences. For the feature value of the context vector, we use the pointwise mutual information (PMI), which provides a measure of the co-occurrence of the keywords and the content words. Performing the complete-link clustering method (furthest neighbor method), we choose the cluster keywords as those yielding high conditional probabilities in Step 2.

3.4 Step 4: Representative phrase selection

For each cluster obtained in Step 3, we select representative phrases from among those containing the keywords, and output them as identified misinformation. To select corrected phrases of suitable length that can provide a sufficient description of the misinformation, we compute the score,

$$\mathrm{Score}_p(s,t) = \mathrm{hist}_t(\mathrm{len_s}) \sum_{\mathrm{w} \in \mathrm{C_s}} \mathrm{PMI}(\mathrm{t},\mathrm{w}), \quad (2)$$

where s denotes the corrected phrase, t denotes the representative keyword of the misinformation cluster, C_s indicates the set of content words in s, and $\mathrm{len_s}$ is the number of words in s. The term $\mathrm{hist}_t(\mathrm{len_s})$ represents the ratio (relative frequency) of occurrences of sentences consisting of $\mathrm{len_s}$ words with the keyword t. $\mathrm{PMI}(t,w)$ represents the pointwise mutual information of the cooccurrence t and w.

Equation 2 is designed to yield a high score for corrected phrases that contain numerous content words that co-occur frequently with the keywords and are of a standard length. In essence, $\mathrm{hist}_t(\mathrm{len_s})$ is a compensatory term that yields a high score for phrases of typical length among those containing the keyword t. For each cluster obtained in Step 3, we choose the phrase $\hat{s}$ yielding the highest score as the representative description for the keyword t.

4 Experiment 1 — CP evaluation

For misinformation acquisition by the proposed method, it is essential to identify CPs that can effectively represent the misinformation. Our first experiment was to evaluate the performance of our CPs.

Table 1: Precision and recall of correction patterns

Precision	Recall
0.79 (118/150)	0.83 (50/60)

4.1 Experimental setting

The corpus that was used as the source of information for the misinformation extraction evaluation comprised 179,286,297 tweets posted between 9:00 JST on March 11 and 9:00 on March 18, 2011, which were provided by Twitter Japan at the Great East Japan Earthquake Big Data Workshop[3]. To create a reference data set, we collected all the instances of misinformation from four misinformation consolidation websites[4] and chose from them 60 instances of misinformation that were determined to have been posted during the week following the Tohoku Earthquake. During the CP performance evaluation, these 60 misinformation instances were compared with approximately 20,000 corrected phrases that were automatically extracted by our CPs. In this evaluation, these 60 instances were denoted as "valid (or gold) instances".

The CPs were evaluated for precision and recall. For precision evaluation, we took 150 samples selected at random from the approximately 20,000 instances of corrected phrases. Precision was defined as the proportion of those samples that were recognized by the CPs as instances of information correction or refutation made by their posters. Recall was defined as the proportion of the 60 valid instances that were recognized from the set of approximately 20,000 instances of corrected phrases.

4.2 Results and analysis

As shown by the values found for the CP precision and recall values in Table 1, the precision and recall values of the misinformation extraction were both approximately 80%. The corrected phrases that were extracted were found to be of four types, as shown in Table 2.

Those in types (a) and (b) were identified as

[3] https://sites.google.com/site/prj311/

[4] The following four websites:
http://www.kotono8.com/2011/04/08dema.html
http://d.hatena.ne.jp/seijotcp/20110312/p1
http://hara19.jp/archives/4905
http://matome.naver.jp/odai/2130024145949727601

Table 2: Types of corrected phrases extracted

Phrase type	#
(a) Having sufficient content for recognition as phrases with corrected information	76
(b) Lacking sufficient content for recognition as phrases with corrected information	42
(c) Phrases erroneously extracted that represent instances of ambiguous patterns	24
(d) Phrases erroneously extracted that represent instances of unclear author intent	8
Total	150

Table 3: Causes of failure to extract misinformation

Cause	#
(e) New correction pattern	3
(f) Evidence present in corrective tweet	4
(g) No corrective tweet	3
Total	10

valid in the evaluation that yielded the results shown in Table 1. Type (b) is of special interest because it comprises phrasing instances in which the misinformation is either not explicitly stated (e.g. "昨日のあれ (That thing yesterday)" in "昨日のあれ ってデマ だったのか (That thing yesterday was a piece of disinformation)", where the CP underlined) or insufficiently expressed (e.g. "that Isodine affair" in "I heard that Isodine affair was a case of disinformation"). Presumably, corrected phrases of type (b) can be eliminated by the conditional probability ranking and representative phrase selection performed by Steps 2 and 4, respectively.

Those of types (c) and (d) were both mistakenly extracted in the evaluation. Type (c) comprises instances of phrasing in which the corrected phrase was extracted by erroneous CP application (e.g., "こういう災害のとき (In times of disaster such as this)" in "こういう災害のとき ってデマ がよく流れる (In times of disaster such as this, disinformation flows freely)"). Type (d) comprises phrases in which the attitude of the writer toward the CP (in regards to the correction) is ambiguous or vague (e.g., "募金するとモテるってデマを流せばいいのに (Fundraising will make you popular - spreading that rumor will have an effect)").

Table 4: Accuracy and recall of extracted misinformation

N	Acc (4-sites)	Acc (manual)	Recall
25	0.44(11/25)	0.64(16/25)	0.18(11/60)
50	0.34(17/50)	0.58(29/50)	0.28(17/60)
75	0.33(25/75)	0.56(42/75)	0.42(25/60)
100	0.30(30/100)	0.52(52/100)	0.50(30/60)

We also examined the 10 instances of failure to extract misinformation and, as shown in Table 6, found the following three types.

Type (e) involved corrective phrasing that was not covered by the existing CPs, such as the underlined portion of the statement, "天皇が 24 時間御祈祷に入ってる ってのはソースがない (No information source is given to show that the Emperor actually performed 24 hours of prayer)". Extraction of this type will be possible with the addition of new CPs. Type (f) comprises types of misinformation correction or refutation that are outside the scope of the CP forms considered in this study. One instance of this is the following corrective tweet, which opposes the disinformation stating that, "日本に韓国が借金の申し出。しかも管は快諾 (South Korea requests loan from Japan. And (P.M.) Kan readily agrees.)"

> "これデマなんじゃ？ ソースないし。RT @xxx RT こんな非常事態の日本に韓国が借金の申し出。しかも管は快諾! (This looks like a fabrication. No source given. RT@xxx. RT. In the present state of emergency, South Korea asks Japan for a loan. And Kan readily agrees!)".

Several tweets intended to correct misinformation were found to take the form of commentary on an original tweet, as in this example.

Type (g) comprises several instances in which tweets purveying misinformation were present among the tweet collection used in this study, but related corrective tweets were not. Extraction of such misinformative tweets by the proposed method would be difficult at best, as our method assumes the occurrence of correction tweets, but such instances were small in number.

5 Experiment 2 — Evaluation of misinformation consolidation

Table 5: Types of errors that lowered accuracy

Error type	#	%
(a) Errors in topic extraction	12	25.0
(b) Errors in clustering 1	20	41.7
(c) Information of uncertain content	5	10.4
(d) Extraction of correct information	1	2.1
(e) Prediction of future events	5	10.4
(f) Validity unclear	5	10.4
Total	48	100.0

Table 6: Types of errors that lowered recall

Error type	#	%
(g) Errors in clustering 2	2	10.0
(h) Low ranking	18	90.0
Total	20	100.0

We next evaluated Steps 2 to 4 of Section 3. This evaluation essentially consisted of determining whether these two steps, when applied to the corrected phrases extracted in Section 4, effectively excluded the type (b) corrected phrases from the extracted phrase set (lacking a statement of the specific information) and whether the selected representative phrases contained appropriate descriptions of misinformation.

5.1 Experimental setting

We assessed the misinformation extracted by the proposed method by manually examining each instance to determine whether it was equivalent in content to any of the 60 gold instances from the four consolidation websites. For some of the misinformation extracted by the proposed method, no similar instances were found in the gold set. In those cases, we manually investigated the information with Web search engines to determine whether it actually was a case of misinformation. Additionally, as the objective in the present study is a comprehensive extraction of misinformation, in cases where the content two or more instances of extracted misinformation were deemed to be essentially the same, we counted them as one correct instance of extraction. Ultimately, the accuracy and recall in this investigation were determined using various values of N, which is the predetermined number of information instances output in order of decreasing score, in the proposed method.

5.2 Experimental results and analysis

Table 4 shows the results of the evaluation. With N as 100, approximately 30% of the information instances extracted by the proposed method were found to be present in the gold set. In addition, approximately 20% of the extracted instances were found to be actual instances of information, and thus correct, even though they were not present in the gold set. Therefore, it can be said that the proposed method extracted misinformation with a precision of approximately 50%. Among the incorrect answers, approximately half involved redundant expressions of essentially the same misinformation phrased differently. In summary, approximately 70% of the misinformation extracted by the proposed method represented a correct answer.

Investigation of the causes of the inaccuracy in output represented by the 48 incorrect answers present among the top 100 extracted misinformation instances showed that they could be classified into six types. These are listed in Table 5, together with the number of incorrect answers attributable to each type. Types (a) to (d) involve instances that were easily judged as errors, but types (e) and (f) involve instances that would be difficult for humans to characterize as either true information or misinformation. The six cause types, and potential means of avoiding them, are as follows:

(a) Errors in keyword extraction In some instances, unsuitable keywords such as "なんちゃら (watchamacallit)", "どさくさ (mess)", and "○ ○ " (a symbol used to mean "a certain", as in "a certain person") were extracted as misinformation keywords. It may be possible to eliminate this source of error in Step 2 by excluding extraction terms that are written entirely in hiragana (the Japanese cursive syllabary) and/or terms composed in large degree of symbols, such as "○ ○ " above.

(b) Errors in clustering Among the top 100 instances of information extraction, some involved redundancies in the form of different phrases that have essentially the same content, as in the following examples, in which the terms in parentheses were theme terms used in the selection process.

市原市のコスモ石油千葉製油所 LPG タンクの爆発により、千葉県、近隣圏に在住の方に有害な雨などと一緒に飛散する(コスモ石油千葉製油所)
(Due to the explosion of the Cosmo

Oil Chiba Refinery LPG tank in Ichihara City, residents of Chiba Prefecture and its neighboring regions will be subjected to toxic rain. (Cosmo Oil Chiba Refinery)
千葉県の石油コンビナート爆発で、空気中に人体に悪影響な物質が空気中に舞い雨が降ると酸性雨になる（石油コンビナート爆発）
Due to the Chiba Prefecture petrochemical complex explosion, the substances adversely affecting human health will mix in the air and fall as acidic rain. (petrochemical complex explosion)

Because these two instances of misinformation were not assigned to the same cluster in Step 3, they gave rise to apparent redundancy. While the current method takes words that co-occur in corrected phrases as their features, it may be possible to reduce this type of redundancy by adding surface information of the keywords themselves to the feature set.

(c) Information of uncertain content This involves instances in which the selected representative phrase states the misinformation inadequately, as in the following example:

餓死者や凍死者が出た。
Death by starvation and freezing has occurred.

The gold set included the sentence "いわき市で餓死者や凍死者が出た (In Iwaki City, death by starvation and freezing have occurred)", but the above representative statement is less specific and was therefore considered to be uncertain in content. Tweets containing such phrases were small in number, and may therefore be excluded by setting a threshold number for this purpose.

(d) Erroneous extraction of true information The following was extracted as misinformation, but when checked against reality was found to be true:

東京タワーの先端が曲がった
The tip of Tokyo Tower has been bent.

When people saw this, many also considered this to be misinformation, as its content seems wildly implausible. However, in the present evaluation, it was the only instance of this type detected among 100 instances of extracted information, and is therefore not considered to be a substantial problem.

(e) Prediction of future events In some instances, expressions comprising the prediction of a future event were extracted, such as the following:

福島で核爆発が起こる
A nuclear explosion will occur in Fukushima.

(f) Unclear validity We found some instances in which a search of several websites yielded no indication of whether they involved misinformation, as in the following example:

サントリーが自販機無料開放
Suntory opens vending machines to dispense products free of charge.

Among the 60 gold instances of misinformation, 20 were included in the corrected phrase set but were not extracted as misinformative. Our investigation into the causes showed that they were of the following two types, which are listed in Table 6 together with the number that occurred in each type.

(g) Errors in clustering In some instances, the candidates were extracted by the CPs but were mistakenly merged with other misinformation instances during the clustering process. However, they apparently do not pose a substantial problem because their number was small in comparison with the total quantity of extracted misinformation.

(h) Unduly low ranking In some instances, candidates were extracted by the CPs but were not extracted as keywords because of their low conditional probability. One example of this is in the misinformation, "東京電力を装った男が現れた (A man pretending to be from Tokyo Electric Power appeared on the scene)". The keyword "Tokyo Electric Power" frequently occurs in statements that do not involve misinformation, and its conditional probability of exhibiting misinformation was therefore estimated to be low. Accordingly, a means of scoring for corrected phrases themselves, rather than for independent keywords, is necessary to eliminate this problem.

6 Conclusion

In this study, we focused on expressions that correct or refute misinformation, and proposed a method for automatic collection of misinformation. The method was evaluated in an experiment during which entries extracted from misinformation consolidation websites that had been manually classified as misinformation were taken as gold instances and used as a basis for comparison with information extracted by the proposed method as misinformation. Some of this extracted misinformation was not listed as misinformation in the consolidation websites, which, together with the other results, showed that the proposed method could be useful for automatic collection of misinformation or, at least, for helping people create and update a comprehensive list of misinformation.

In our future studies, we intend to work to expand the set of CPs used in this method and to improve the corrected phrase scoring, thereby enhancing its performance in misinformation extraction, together with the development of a complete system for real-time misinformation acquisition.

Acknowledgments

This study was partly supported by Japan Society for the Promotion of Science (JSPS) KAKENHI Grants No. 23240018 and 23700159 and by the Precursory Research for Embryonic Science and Technology (PREST), Japan Science and Technology Agency (JST). We are grateful to Twitter Japan for its provision of invaluable data. Finally, we wish to thank the workshop organizers, who gave the opportunity to present and discuss important applications of natural language processing that help people in disaster situations.

References

Tomohide Fujikawa, Nobuhiro Kaji, Naoki Yoshinaga, and Masaru Kitsuregawa. 2012. Classsification of users' attitudes toward rumors on microblogs. In *Technical Report of the Institute of Electronics, Information and Communication Engineers*.

Mai Miyabe, Ayana Umejima, Akiyo Nadamoto, and Eiji Aramaki. 2012. Ryugenjoho cloud: Collecting false rumors by extracting correction information from humans. In *Proceedings of the 18th Annual Meeting of the Association for Natural Language Processing*, pages 891–894.

Ltd. Nomura Research Institute. 2011. Survey on "trends in people's use and views of media in the wake of the tohoku - pacific ocean earthquake". `http://www.nri.co.jp/english/news/2011/110329.html`.

Vahed Qazvinian, Emily Rosengren, Dragomir R. Radev, and Qiaozhu Mei. 2011. Rumor has it: identifying misinformation in microblogs. In *Proceedings of the Conference on Empirical Methods in Natural Language Processing*, EMNLP '11, pages 1589–1599, Stroudsburg, PA, USA. Association for Computational Linguistics.

Fujio Toriumi, Kosuke Shinoda, and Genta Kaneyama. 2012. Evaluating a system that judges false rumors in social media. *Journal of Digital Practice*, 3(3):201–208.

Ayana Umejima, Mai Miyabe, Akiyo Nadamoto, and Eiji Aramaki. 2011. Tendency of rumor and correction re-tweet on the twitter during disasters. In *IPSJ SIG Technical Report*, volume 2011, pages 1–6.

Ayana Umejima, Mai Miyabe, Akiyo Nadamoto, and Eiji Aramaki. 2012. Analysis for extracting rumor markers in microblogs. In *Proceedings of DEIM Forum 2012*, pages F3–2.

Returning-Home Analysis in Tokyo Metropolitan Area at the time of the Great East Japan Earthquake using Twitter Data

Yusuke Hara
New Industry Creation Hatchery Center, Tohoku University
6-3-09 Aoba Aramaki Aoba-ku Sendai, Miyagi 980-8579, Japan
hara@plan.civil.tohoku.ac.jp

Abstract

This paper clarifies the occurrence factors of commuters unable to return home and the returning-home decision-making at the time of the Great East Japan Earthquake by using Twitter data. First, to extract the behavior data from the tweet data, we identify each user's returning-home behavior using support vector machines. Second, we create non-verbal explanatory factors using geotag data and verbal explanatory factors using tweet data. Then, we model users' returning-home decision-making by using a discrete choice model and clarify the factors quantitatively. Finally, by sensitivity analysis, we show the effects of the existence of emergency evacuation facilities and line of communication.

1 Introduction

The 2011 earthquake off the Pacific coast of Tohoku, often referred to in Japan as the Great East Japan Earthquake, was a magnitude 9.0 under sea megathrust earthquake that occurred at 14:46JST (05:46 UTC) on March 11, 2011. The focal region of this earthquake was widespread, spanning approximately 500 km north to south from off the Ibaraki shore to the Iwate shore and approximately 200km east to west. The number of deaths and missing persons attributed to this disaster totaled more than 19,000, and the complex, large-scale disasters of the earthquake, tsunami, and nuclear power plant accident had a major impact on people's lives. The Tokyo metropolitan area also was hit by a strong earthquake and various traffic problems occurred. For example, many railway and subway services were suspended for maintenance. Therefore, almost every railway and subway user was unable to return home easily, and they were called "victims unable to return home." According to (Measures Council for Victims Unable to Return Home by Earthquake that directly hits Tokyo Area, 2012), the number of people who were not able to go home during that day by paralysis of these transport networks is estimated about 5.15 million people and it is 30% of a going-out people of the day.

Assessing the problem of "victims unable to return home" in Tokyo metropolitan area is extremely important for anti-disaster measures. Although the questionnaire is performed ex post, it is not yet shown clearly what made going-home decision-making after the earthquake disaster. Moreover, since it was going-home behavior in big confusion, the problem that detailed time and position information are unknown exist.

Some previously studies have examined human behaviors via analysis of behavior log data at the time of a large-scale disaster. Because no rapid and accurate method existed to track population movements after the 2010 earthquake in Haiti, (Bengtsson et al., 2011) used position data from subscriber identity module (SIM) cards from the largest mobile phone company in Haiti to estimate the magnitude and trends of population movements after the 2010 Haiti earthquake and the subsequent cholera outbreak. Their results indicated that estimates of population movements during disasters and outbreaks can be acquired rapidly and with potentially high validity in areas of high mobile phone usage. (Lu et al., 2012) also used the same data in Haiti to determine that 19 days after the earthquake, population movements had caused the population of the capital Port-au-Prince to decrease by approximately 23% and that the destinations of people who left the capital during the first three weeks after the earthquake were highly correlated with their mobility patterns during normal times and specifically with the locations of people with whom they had significant social bonds. Lu et al. concluded that population movements during disasters may be significantly more predictable than previously thought. Overall, these previous studies clarified human movement over long periods of time. They showed that people in areas affected by an earthquake take refuge temporarily and that the population in the affected area is recovered over several months. Behavior log data should be able to clarify not only such long-term human behavior but also the human behaviors at the time of a disaster.

In this research, we analyze tweet data of Twitter as the behavior log data at the time of the Great East Japan Earthquake. Although tweet data does not contain actual behavior necessarily, there is possibility of containing thinking process and behavioral factors. We clarify the factors of going-home behavior in case of the Great East Japan Earthquake using Twitter data.

2 From Tweet Data To Behavioral Data

2.1 Framework

First, we provide a framework of this research to analyze users' going-home behavior using tweet data and geotag data. Figure 1 shows our framework: (1) behavior inference by tweet data,(2) feature engineering by geotag and tweet data, (3) estimation of behavioral model.

In (1) behavior inference by tweet data part, we inferred users' going-home behavior result using Support vector machine (SVM) and Bag-Of-Words (BOW) representation. In (2) feature engineering by geotag and tweet data part, we made explanatory factors of users' behavior from tweet data and geotag data. In (3) estimation of behavioral model part, we estimated users' behavior model (discrete choice model).

2.2 Data

In this section, we provide an outline of our data. This data is about 180-million tweet by Japanese in Twitter from March 11, 2011 to March 18, 2011. There are about 280 thousands tweet with geotag in this data. We sampled tweets whose timestamp is from 14:00, March 11 to 10:00, March 12 and whose GPS location is within Tokyo metropolitan area. The number of these tweet is 24,737 and the number of unique users (account) is 5,281. To observe users' trip on the day, we extracted users that had over 2 geotag tweet and the number of users is 3,307. We assume that these users can tweet about the Great East Japan Earthquake and their going-home behavior. Therefore, we analyzed all tweet of these users from 14:00, March 11 to 10:00 (3,307 users, 132, 989 tweets).

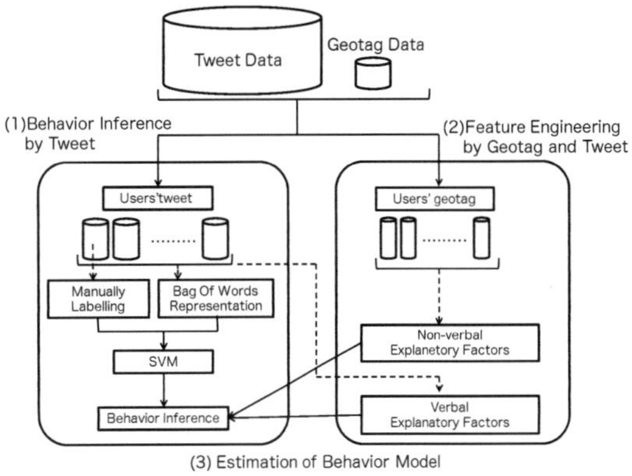

Figure 1: Framework in this research

We tagged 300 users' going-home behavior result manually to make supervised data. Our label set is composed of 1) going home by foot, 2) by train, 3) staying their offices or hotels until tomorrow morning, 4) other choice (taxi, bus, etc.), 5) unclear.

2.3 Morphological analysis

Next, we give morphological analysis by MeCab and obtained BOW representation by each user's tweet. To find the relationship between going-home behavior and each user's tweet, we use information gain. Information gain is index which shows decreasing degree of each class's entropy by existing word w. If word w is contained each user's tweet, Random variableX_w equals 1 and otherwise $X_w = 0$. Random variables which indicates each class is c and entropy $H(c)$ is written as

$$H(C) = -\sum_c P(c) \log P(c). \quad (1)$$

And conditional entropy is written as

$$H(c|X_w = 1) = -\sum_c P(c|X_w = 1) \log P(c|X_w = 1)$$
$$H(c|X_w = 0) = -\sum_c P(c|X_w = 0) \log P(c|X_w = 0).$$

Information gain $IG(w)$ of word w is defined as average decreasing entropy and written as

$$IG(w) = H(c) - (P(X_w = 1)H(c|X_w = 1) + P(X_w = 0)H(c|X_w = 0)) \quad (2)$$

Table 1: Illustrative examples of words whose information gain is high

1)by foot	駅 (station) 歩い (walk) 足 (foot) 休憩 (rest) 自転車 (bicycle) 電車 (train) ヤバイ (danger) 止まっ (stop) 半分 (half) 到着 (arrived) 歩ける (can walk) テレビ (TV) トイレ (toilet) 環七 (Kan-nana Street) km 川崎 (Kawasaki) 疲れ (tired) 遠い (far) 道 (road)
2)by train	大江戸 (O-edo subway line) 入場 (entry) 田園都市線 (Denen-toshi line) 奇跡 (miracle) なんとか (luckily) 順調 (smoothly) 京王 (Keio line) 乗れ (can take a train)
3)stay	泊め (sleep) 朝 (morning) 総武線 (Sobu line) 混雑 (congested) 検索 (search) JR (JR line) 乗車 (take a train) 満員 (full capacity) 明け (daylight) 暇 (a spare time) 始発 (first train in the morning) 悩む (worry)
4)other	Twitpic
5)unclear	jishin, skype

We calculated all words information gain $IG(w)$ by 5 class (walk, train, stay, other, unclear). Table 1 shows illustrative examples. For example, words whose conditional probability of walking is high are “half”, “far”, “km”, “Kawasaki” and “Kannana Street”. They show user’s location. And “toilet”, “tired” and “danger” indicates psychological factors during going-home by foot.

In the case of train, “miracle”, “luckily” is contained and “O-edo line” and “Denen-toshi line” are the train and subway lines which is operated in March 11. In the case of stay, “morning”, “daylight” and “sleep” indicates that users slept at hotel or their offices and “first train in the morning”, “worry” and “search” shows their going-home timing. Other choices users, who choose bicycle, taxi etc, and unclear users don’t show the understandable tendency. However, they submitted pictures for Twitpic, which is photo share site, and tweeted with #jishin hashtag.

As seen above, the words whose information gain is high is useful to infer their going-home behavior. Therefore, we made classifier by using these words as features.

2.4 SVM and behavior inference

In this section, we infer each user’s behavioral result by SVM. we use 300 labeled data as supervised data and we treat top 500 words of information gain as features of SVM. In learning, we did 9-fold cross validation and average accuracy rate is 73.3%.

Figure 2 shows the inferred result. The number

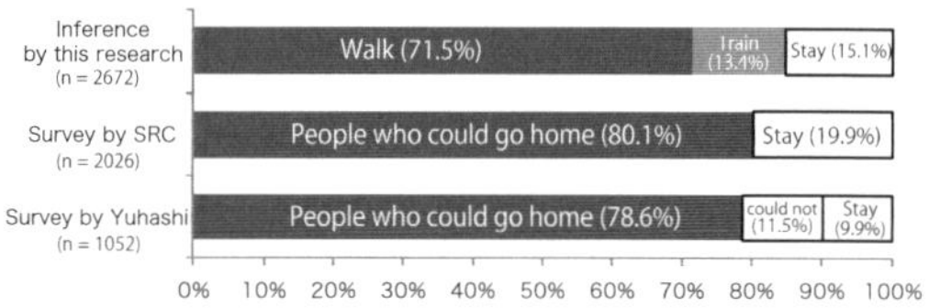

Figure 2: Inferred result and comparison of other survey

of users by foot is $1,913$, the number of users by train is 359, the number of users staying is 385, the number of users by other choice is 15 and the number of users whose choice is unclear is 635. This result indicates that the ratio of all going-home users except unclear users is $84,9\%$.

To discuss the accuracy of this inference result, we compare our result with other survey results. Figure 2 shows the survey result by (Survey Research Center, 2011) and the survey result by (Yuhashi, 2012). The result of Survey Research Center says 80.1% of all could get home and the result of Yuhashi says 78.6% of all could get home.

3 Behavioral Analysis

3.1 Non-verval factors

Based on the prediction of going-home decision-making classified by user, nonverbal / verbal explanation factor is created from tweet data or geotag data, and the factor of each individual’s going-home decision-making is analyzed.

First, the explanation factor about travel behavior is created using the geotag data classified by user. In this research, for simplicity, we assume that a position before the earthquake is the location of office (origin) and a position of 12:00, March 12, 2011 is the location of home (destination). Next, road network distance, the on foot time required, the station nearest office, the station nearest home, the railroad time required, railroad expense, and the number of times of a railroad change are created using these GPS data. These are the features created using the network at the time of usual.

In order to express a spatial spread of people’s going-home behavior, Figure 3, 4 shows the spatial dstribution of users’ location of before the earthquake and the next day of the earthquake by plotting each user’s geotag. As an overall trend, office distribution and house distribution are spatially different, and home distribution is spread in

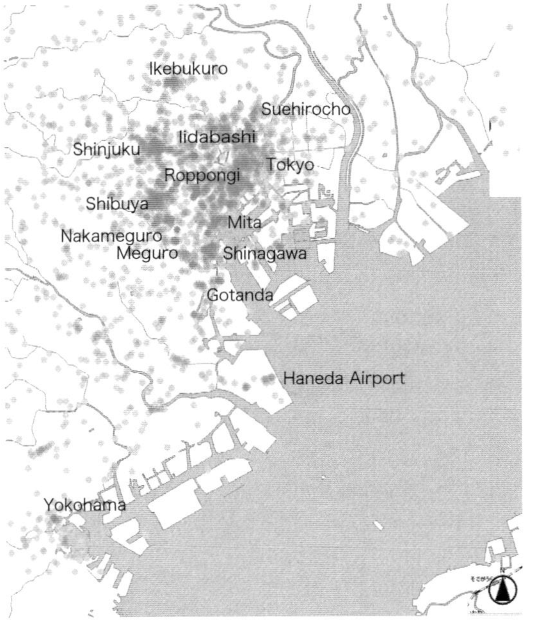

Figure 3: Users' location distribution before the earthquake

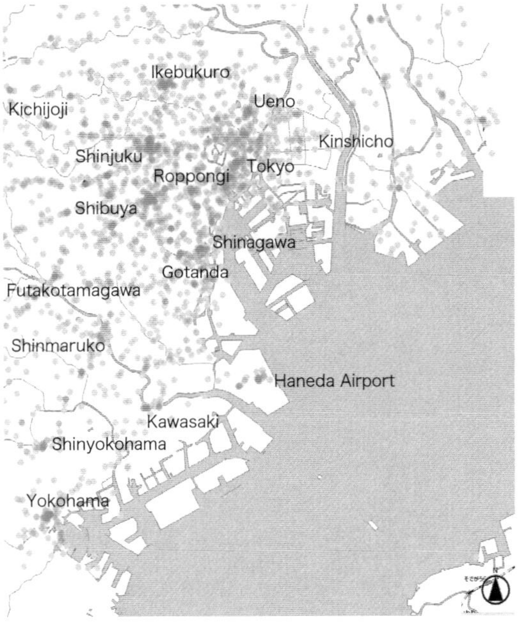

Figure 4: Users' location distribution in the morning on March 12

the direction of the suburban area.

Next, the cross tabulation result of going-home decision-making by the road network distance between offices and houses is shown in Figure 5. This result indicates that the rate of on foot decreases relatively as distance with a house becomes long, but 50% or more of people got home on foot if their distance is 20 km over.

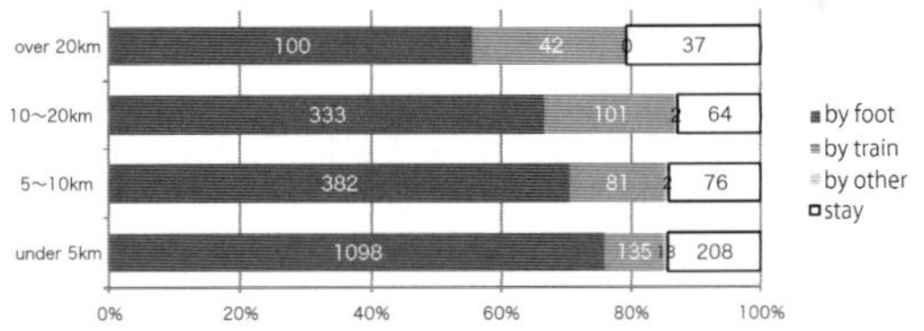

Figure 5: The relationship between going-home behavior and the distance

3.2 Verbal factors

Finally, a verbal explanation factor is generated. Since it is surmised that a family's existence and with or without information has affected going-home decision-making, the factor which affects going-home decision-making behavior is extracted from each user's tweet.

First, we analyze the effect of a safety check with a family. In this research, the family was defined as a spouse and children living together. And 353 of 3,307 persons had spoken existence of a family living together. We extracted safety check tweet such as "I got e-mail from my wife! I felt easy,", "The telephone led to the wife and the daughter at last! " and "My telephone is not connected to my son's nursery school. "

Figure 6, 7 shows the time zone rate of the safety checked tweet and the safety unidentified tweet according to going-home decision making.

Safety checked tweets are concentrated before 18:00 (42% of on foot, 45% of by train, and 65% of stay). Safety unidentified tweets are also concentrated before 18:00. We assume that the safety unidentified tweets are strongly reflecting each individual's psychological state because they can perform every time zone until safety checked. If we assume that the tweet in a earlier time zone is more important for each user, an on foot going-home person will regard his/her family's safety unidentified situation as more questionable than a railroad going-home person, and he may make decision of going-home by foot.

Next, the relationship between the information of train operation again and going-home decision-making is analyzed. The train line on the day was resumed one by one after 20:40. It is dependent on the acquisition existence of railroad resumption information whether he stays in his office or he goes home using the resumed railroad. Figure 8 shows the relationship between the rate of rail-

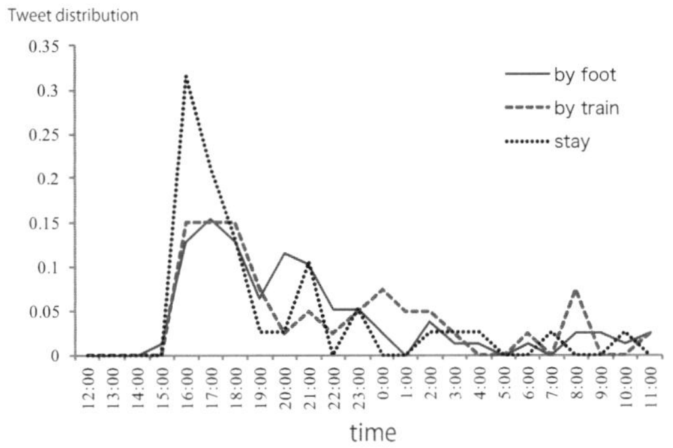

Figure 6: The distribution of safety checked tweets

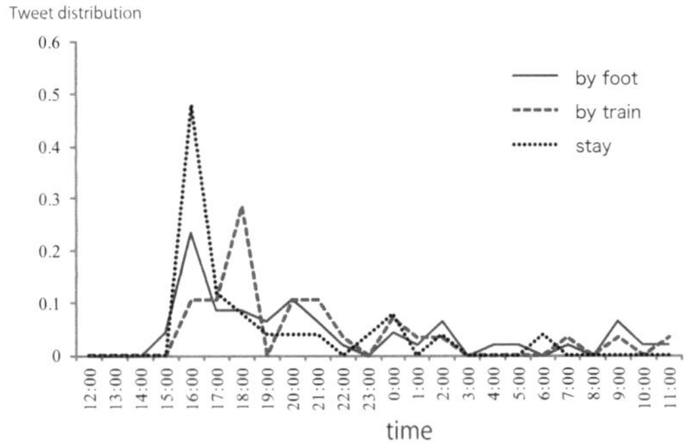

Figure 7: The distribution of safety unidentified tweets

road resumption tweet and going-home decision-making and it indicates that a railroad chooser tend to speak of railroad resumption information.

Finally, we analyze the relationship between individual psychological factor and going-home decision-making. On March 11, many utterances about their mental situation were seen. Figure 9 shows the utterance rate of uneasy and going-home decision-making result. Interestingly, individuals whose utterance rate of uneasy is under 5% tend to stay at office or hotel but people whose utterance rate of uneasy is over 5% tend to go home by foot. This results shows the person who felt fear tend to walk to home.

4 Behavioral Model

4.1 Discrete choice model

We built discrete choice model based on the explanatory variable generated in **3**. Discrete choice model is a statistical model used in fields, such as econometrics, travel behavior analysis, and marketing, and is also called Random utility model ((Ben-Akiva and Lerman, 1985); (Train, 2003)). In this research, Multinomial Logit Model (MNL) is used and it is the most fundamental model in a discrete choice model.

Discrete choice models describe decision mak-

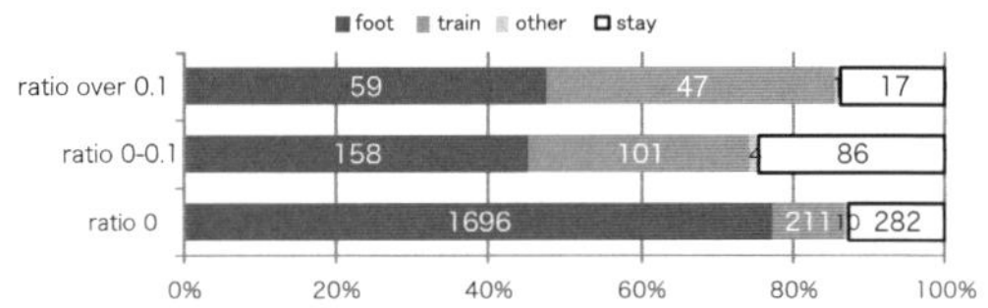

Figure 8: The relationship between the rate of railroad resumption tweet and going-home decision-making

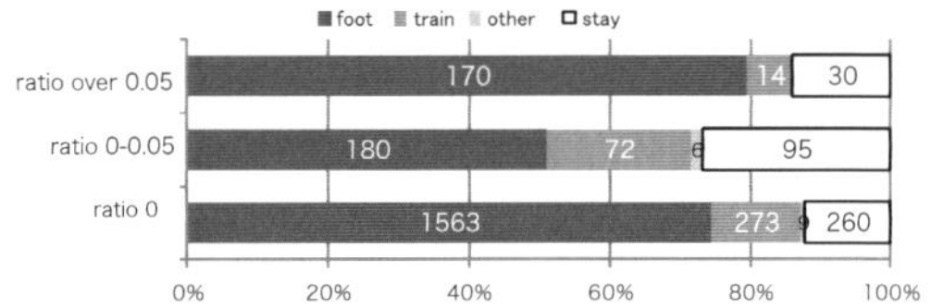

Figure 9: The relationship between uneasy tweet and going-home decision-making

ers' choices among alternatives. A decision maker, labeled n, faces a choice among J alternatives. The decision maker would obtain a certain level of utility from each alternative. The utility that decision maker n obtains from alternative j is $U_{nj},\ j = 1, \ldots, J$. This utility is known to the decision maker but not, as we see in the following, by the researcher. The decision maker chooses the alternative that provides the greatest utility. The behavioral model is therefore: choose alternative i if and only if $U_{ni} > U_{nj},\ \forall j \neq i$.

Consider now the researcher. The researcher does not observe the decision maker's utility. The researcher observes some attributes of the alternatives as faced by the decision maker, labeled $x_{nj}\ \forall j$, and some attributes of the decision maker, labeled s_n, and can specify a function that relates these observed factors to the decision maker's utility. The function is denoted $V_{nj} = V(x_{nj}, s_n)\ \forall j$ and is often called representative utility. Usually, V depends on parameters that are unknown to the researcher and therefore estimated statistically.

Since there are aspects of utility that the researcher does not or cannot observe, $V_{nj} = U_{nj}$. Utility is decomposed as $U_{nj} = V_{nj} + \varepsilon_{nj}$, where ε_{nj} captures the factors that affect utility but are not included in V_{nj}. This decomposition is fully general.

The researcher does not know $\varepsilon_{nj}\ \forall j$ and therefore treats these terms as random. The joint density of the random vector $\varepsilon_n = (\varepsilon_{n1}, \ldots, \varepsilon_{nJ})$ is denoted $f(\varepsilon_{nj})$. With this density, the researcher can make probabilistic statements about the decision maker's choice. The probability that decision maker n chooses alternative i is

$$\begin{aligned} P_{ni} &= \Pr(U_{ni} > U_{nj} \ \forall j \neq i) \\ &= \Pr(V_{ni} + \varepsilon_{ni} > V_{nj} + \varepsilon_{nj} \ \forall j \neq i) \\ &= \Pr(V_{ni} - V_{nj} > \varepsilon_{nj} - \varepsilon_{ni} \ \forall j \neq i) \quad (3) \end{aligned}$$

This probability is a cumulative distribution, namely, the probability that each random term $\varepsilon_{nj} - \varepsilon_{ni}$ is below the observed quantity $V_{ni} - V_{nj}$. MNL model is derived under the assumption that the unobserved portion of utility is distributed iid extreme value.

$$f(\varepsilon_{nj}) = e^{-\varepsilon_{nj}} e^{-e^{-\varepsilon_{nj}}} \quad (4)$$

$$F(\varepsilon_{nj}) = e^{-e^{-\varepsilon_{nj}}} \quad (5)$$

And decision maker n chooses alternative i is derived as

$$P_{ni} = \frac{e^{V_{ni}}}{\sum_j e^{V_{nj}}}. \quad (6)$$

This is choice probability of MNL model.

4.2 The setting of utility function

In discrete choice model, observed utility term V_{ni} is generally defined as $V_{ni} = \boldsymbol{\beta}' \boldsymbol{x}_{ni}$. $\boldsymbol{\beta}$ is coefficient vector and $\boldsymbol{x}_{ni}$ is explanatory vector of decision maker n's alternative i.

In this research, data set is 2672 samples identified by SVM except persons unclear and choice set is on foot, train, other and stay. Explanatory variables of on foot are required time by foot, the ratio of uneasy tweets and alternative specific constant. Explanatory variables of train are required time by train, log of the distance between office and home, the ratio of train resumption tweets, the dummy variables of family safety checked tweets and alternative specific constant. Explanatory variables of stay are the ratio of uneasy tweets, the ratio of waiting position tweets, the dummy variables of family safety checked tweets and alternative specific constant. We normalized the utility of other to 0.

Next, we outlines the estimation method of the coefficient parameter of a utility function. MNL model's likelihood function is written as

$$LL(\beta) = \sum_{n=1}^{N} \sum_{i} \delta_{ni} \ln P_{ni} \quad (7)$$

where δ_{ni} is Kronecker delta if decision maker n choice i, $\delta_{ni} = 1$ and otherwise $\delta_{ni} = 0$. This likelihood function is globally concave (McFadden, 1974). Therefore, parameters can be estimated uniquely with a maximum likelihood estimation.

Table 2: The estimation result of MNL model

variables	estimator	t-value
required time (min/10) [foot, train]	-0.012	-2.20
log(distance(km)) [train]	0.36	5.50
the ratio of train resumption [train]	4.17	5.72
the ratio of train uneasy [foot]	6.05	2.71
the ratio of train uneasy [stay]	4.52	1.82
the ratio of waiting position [stay]	2.98	4.52
family safety checked [train, stay]	1.14	3.54
alternative specific constant [foot]	4.88	18.50
alternative specific constant [train]	2.46	8.48
alternative specific constant [stay]	3.08	11.61
observations	2672	
initial log likelihood	-3704.179	
final log likelihood	-2107.771	
likelihood ratio index($\overline{\rho}^2$)	0.428	

4.3 the results and simulation

Under the above setting, the estimation result is shown in Table 2. A likelihood ratio index is 0.428 and its goodness of fit is good enough. Moreover, the result that the coefficient parameter of the required time is negative and the choice probability of train increases as the distance between office and home is far is suitable for basic analysis and intuition,

Moreover, we estimated parameters of the rate of the uneasy tweet separately by on foot and stay. It turns out that the uneasy tweet rate has had bigger influence to on foot choice. For example, from the ratio of parameters, the increase of 5 point uneasy tweet ratio is equivalent to the increase of 64 minutes required time by foot. From a perspective of family safety check, decision maker who could check family's safety tend to choice stay. Therefore, family's safety check is the important factors for the avoidance of confusion at the great disaster.

A sensitivity analysis is conducted based on this result. One is the analysis of the effect of the existence of a stay place on going-home behavior and another is the analysis of effect of family's safety check in the early time zone. Figure 10 shows the results.

First, we consider the case where all people have the waiting place. If the ratio of waiting position tweets of users who choose by foot, train and other is same as the average ratio by stay choosers, the number of choice staying will increase by 1.18

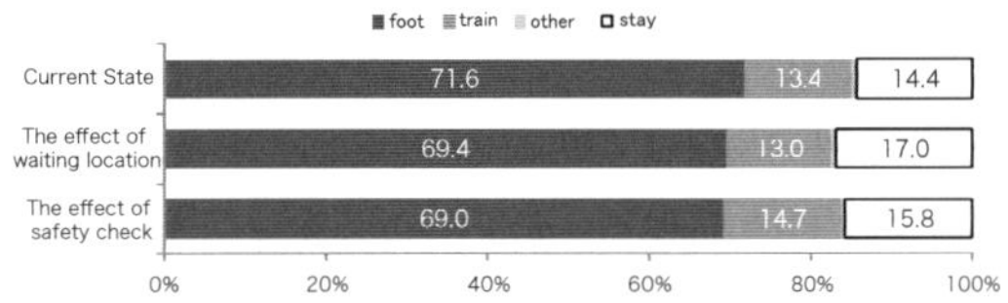

Figure 10: The result of sensitivity analysis

times and the share of stay is 17.0%.

On the other hand, the share of going-home behavior such as on foot and train decreases by 3%. Although 3% of reduction seems to be very small influence apparently, generally the traffic congestion and confusion in a transport system occur by exceeding only 10 % of supplied capacity. From this point, 3% of reduction effects is not few.

Next, we analyzed the influence of the safety check within a family. It is checked from the tweets that there are 353 decision makers who have family living together. When all of these 353 persons was able to check family's safety by 17:00, as shown in Figure 10, the number of agents who choice train or stay increase by 1.1 times, and the number of people who go home by foot decrease by 0.95 time. Needless to say, the safety check within a family at the time of a disaster is the important information. Since lines of communication other than a mobile phone carried out the big contribution by this earthquake disaster, these communication tools can prevent the confusion of transport network partially.

5 Conclusions

In this paper, we inferred the going-home behavior in Tokyo metropolitan area after the Great East Japan Earthquake using tweet data and geotag data of Twitter and clarified the decision-making factors. Although the inference method of going-home behavior and the behavioral model were the existing techniques, by combining two data sources and techniques, the going-home behavior for each individual and its factors were clarified only from Twitter data. And the virtual scenario simulation was carried out and we analyzed the effect of waiting space and communication tools.

In the ex post survey about the behavior in the earthquake disaster, the orders of samples is about thousands of people. In this research, the number of users whose tweets were with geotag is 3,307 people in Tokyo metropolitan area and it is also same order. However, if we can calculate the similarity of users who have geotag and not have geotag from the similarity of users' tweet, human behaviors in the great disaster can be clarified in hundreds thousands of people's order. We would like to consider these approach as future tasks.

Acknowledgments

We specially thank the Great East Japan Earthquake Big Data Workshop and Twitter Japan.

References

Ben-Akiva, M. and Lerman, S. 1985. *Discrete Choice Analysis: Theory and Application to Travel Demand.* MIT Press, Cambridge, MA.

Bengtsson, L., Lu, X., Thorson, A., Garfield, R., von Schreeb, J. 2011. Improved Response to Disasters and Outbreaks by Tracking Population Movements with Mobile Phone Network Data: A Post-Earthquake Geospatial Study in Haiti. *PLoS Medicine*, 8(8), e1001083.

Lu, X., Bengtsson, L. and Holme, P. 2012. Predictability of population displacement after the 2010 Haiti earthquake. *Proceedings of the National Academy of Sciences of the United States of America*, 109(29), 11576–11581.

McFadden, D. 1974. Conditional logit analysis of qualitative choice behavior. *Frontiers in Econometrics*, Academic Press, New York, 105–142.

MeCab Yet Another Part-of-Speech and Morphological Analyzer, http://mecab.sourceforge.net/.

Train, K. 2003. *Discrete Choice Methods with Simulation.* Cambridge University Press, Cambridge.

Survey Research Center. 2011. Survey of the Great East Japan Earthquake disaster ("victims unable toreturn home"). http://www.surece.co.jp/src/press/backnumber/20110407.html.

Measures Council for Victims Unable to Return Home by Earthquake that directly hits Tokyo Area. 2012. Measures Council for Victims Unable to Return Home by Earthquake that directly hits Tokyo Area Final Report. http://www.bousai.metro.tokyo.jp/japanese/tmg/kitakukyougi.htm.

Yuhashi, H, 2012. Returning-Home Situation and Information Behavior in the Great East Japan Earthquake. Japan Society for Disaster Information Studies 14th workshop. A-4-2. 140–143.

BahaBa: A Route Generator System for Mobile Devices

Ralph Vincent J. Regalado, Michael Benedict Y. Haw, Matthew Alexis P. Martinez, Lowie O. Santiaguel, Patrick Lawrence S. Tamayo
Center for Language Technologies
De La Salle University
Manila, Philippines
ralph.regalado@delasalle.ph, {michael_haw, matthew_martinez, lowie_santiaguel, patrick_lawrence_tamayo}@dlsu.ph,

Abstract

The Philippines is considered to be one of the world's most disaster prone countries. Since the use of mobile devices continues to grow, many generated applications for mobile devices that will aid during disaster. While most of the people residing in the urban areas are mostly smartphone users, people who are living in the rural areas are still using low-cost phones. In order to equally provide information that will be needed on or during disaster, we created BahaBa a SMS-based route generation system targeted for mobile devices. The system accepts a SMS and generates a template-based response to the sender, containing instructions on the shortest path to the nearest safe place in a community.

1 Introduction

According to the Asia Pacific Disaster Report 2012, the average number of people in Asia-Pacific who are at risk from yearly flooding doubled from 29.5 million to 63.8 million (United Nations Economic and Social Commission for Asia and the Pacific and United Nations Office for Disaster Risk Reduction, 2012). Philippine is one of the region's hardest hit countries in the past decade which recorded 182 disasters that killed almost 11,000 people (United Nations Office for Disaster Risk Reduction, 2012).

Since the use of mobile devices continues to grow, several local applications for mobile devices have been developed, such as iTyphoon (Nueva Caceres Technology Solutions, Inc., 2013) and Project NOAH (Department of Science and Technology, 2013) , to aid during disasters. Most of these applications require the use of smartphones and mobile internet to contribute and retrieve content.

According to a World Bank (2012) report, Philippines have a high access and usage statistics in mobile communication when compared to other countries. It is highlighted that mobile internet usage in the Philippines is low, 23.1% of Filipino mobile users have mobile broadband connection and only 9.8% use mobile internet. The data also showed that 97% of the users use Short Message Service (SMS). In order to provide information that will be needed on or during disaster we created BahaBa, route generation system targeted for mobile devices. It uses SMS to accept user request and generates a template-based response to the sender containing instructions on the shortest path to the nearest safe place in a community.

The remainder of this paper is organized as follow. Section 2 reviews existing works related to our approaches. Section 3 introduces the main processes of our approach. Section 4 describes our testing results. In Section 5, we conclude our efforts and discuss some future works.

2 Related Literature

The work of Dale, et al. (2003) was one of the early works who used Natural Language Generation (NLG) to provide navigational assistance. Their work, Coral, generate descriptions for routes from an area to another area. Routes generated consider the mode of navigation, means of communication and type of environment. The system represented the world as nodes, arcs and polygons. The nodes represent junctions or decision points, arcs represent travelable paths and polygons represent areas like parks, stations and the like. The system also has several options which allows user to customize their route, whether he wants the shortest or fastest path, avoid an area, or traverse a one way road. The NLG task in Coral involves text planning, micro planning and linguistic realization. Text planning is about taking a path-based route plan that derives messages that are sent to the user. Micro planning makes a list of sentences and identifies what information to be used for the route to be undertaken. Linguistic realization maps the sentences. Same as Coral, our work focuses on using NLG to generate route to safe places. Our NLG task is focus on Text Planning, Discourse Planning and Linguistic Realization.

Fajardo & Oppus (2010) discussed MyDisasterDroid, an application that determines the optimum route to find different ge-graphical locations that the rescuers will take in order to serve effectively during a disaster. In determining the most optimum route along different geographical locations, it was solved as a travelling salesman problem wherein the objective is to go to a location and proceed to another in the shortest way possible in terms of length or cost. Since our work provides a path to a nearest safe place, we used A* search algorithm. This algorithm ensures that a path can be found, and, if it exists, takes distance into consideration as the cost in order achieve the optimal route.

3 The Bahaba System

The BahaBa system is consists of 3 main modules: SMS Processing, Route Generation and Text Generation. Figure 1 shows the system architecture.

3.1 SMS Processing Module

This module is responsible for sending and receiving SMS to and from the user. Once an SMS is received this module validates first the format. The format is:

BHB [Type] [Hazard] [User Location]

BHB is the system key variable. The *[type]* is the keyword for safe places being searched by the user. *[Hazard]* is the keyword if the user wants to consider the surrounding flood hazards. While the *[User Location]*, contains the user's current location. Table 1 and 2 shows the keywords used for *[type]* and *[hazard]*.

Keyword	Description
EC	Evacuation Center
P	Police Station
H	Hospital
O	Any nearest safe place

Table 1. Keywords for Safe Place

Keyword	Description
H	With hazards
NH	Without hazards

Table 2. Keywords for Hazard

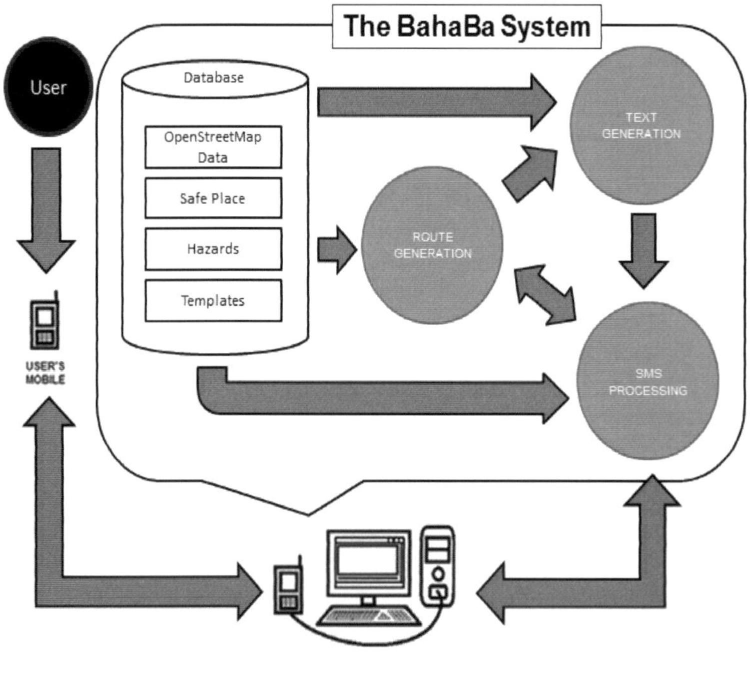

Figure 1. BahaBa System Architecture

Once the format is validated, it will perform location validation. The *[User Location]* will be compared to all the list of locations stored in the database. Once validated, it will transfer the SMS data, and the longitude and latitude of the *[User Location]* to the next module; else it will respond back to the user notifying that the SMS is invalid.

3.2 Route Generation Module

This module handles the actual generation of the route in the form of a list of nodes. It first creates a start node for the start location based on the [User Location]. It then searches the database for a list of safe places specified in the [Type] and creates goal nodes for them.

The task of this module is to look for the nearest safe place from the start location. We treated this route generation as a search problem where, from the initial node, or the start location, the search algorithm finds the fastest and lowest cost path to the goal node, or the target location. We used A* search algorithm since it ensures that a solution or path can be found, and, if it exists, takes distance into consideration as the cost in order achieve the optimal route.

For the evaluation *function f(n)* used in A* search algorithm, the cost *function g(n)* will be the collective cost or distance from the start node to the node *n*, while the heuristic *function h(n)* will be the cost or straight line distance from the node *n* to the goal node. Distances are calculated with the Euclidean distance formula using latitude and longitude as the ordered pair for the nodes as seen in Figure 2.

$$d = \sqrt[2]{\left(latitude(n_1) - latitude(n_2)\right)^2 + \left(longitude(n_1) - longitude(n_2)\right)^2}$$

Figure 2. Euclidian Distance Formula

Since our system consider flood hazards, they are treated as expensive nodes depending on the hazard level. To be more specific, a hazard node can still be a viable node to pass through in a route. To emulate the added cost of a hazard node's flood level, the node's heuristic value can be increased by a value corresponding to the intensity of the flood level. A hazard node that currently has minimal flood levels would have its heuristic increased by a trivial amount, like an additional 10m, which would keep its overall cost lower, while a hazard node that currently has dangerous flood levels would have its heuristic increased by a major amount, like an additional 500m, which would make the node extremely costly to traverse, effectively ruling it out as a possible node in the route. After the shortest path to the goal node is found the module then generates a Text Plan.

The Text Plan is constructed by traversing the route's nodes. Using the location's longitude and latitude found in each node, it identifies if it is traversing a single street and detects when the path turns to a new street or encounters a location landmark. Figure 3 shows an example of a generated Text Plan.

```
De La Salle University {
   nextNode: Dagonoy;
   safePlace: 0;
   hazard: 0;
   landmark: none;
   turn: right;
}
        ↓
Dagonoy {
   nextNode: Leon Guinto;
   safePlace: 0;
   hazard: 0;
   landmark: none;
   turn: left;
}
        ↓
Leon Guinto{
   nextNode: Quirino Avenue;
   safePlace: 0;
   hazard: 0;
   landmark: none;
   turn: left;
}
        ↓
Quirino Avenue {
   nextNode: Ospital ng Maynila;
   safePlace: 0;
   hazard: 0;
   landmark: none;
   turn: right;
}
        ↓
Ospital ng Maynila {
   nextNode: none;
   safePlace: 1;
   hazard: 0;
   landmark: none;
   turn: none;
}
```

Figure 3. Sample Text Plan

If there is a route generated the Text Plan will be passed to the Text generation module; else it will pass it to the SMS processing module to inform the sender that there are no routes available.

3.3 Text Generation Module

This module converts the route generated by the previous module into text form through the use of template-based NLG. This module has two sub-modules: Discourse Planning and Linguistic Realization. Figure 3 shows the process of the Text Generation Module

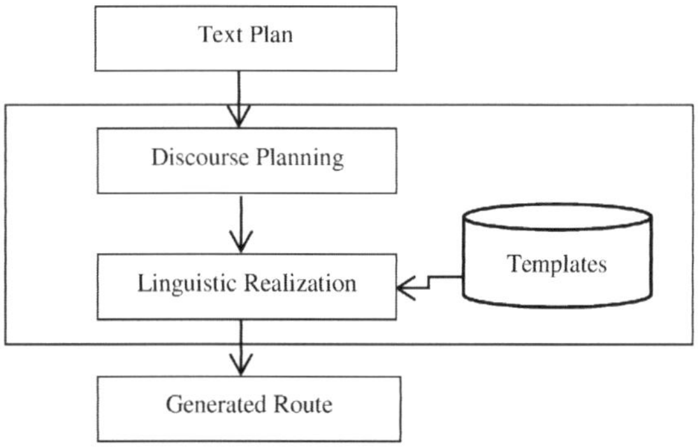

Figure 4. Text Generation Module

Discourse Planning

Each element in the Text Plan is analyzed and categorized according to the templates. Table 3 shows the list of template tag.

Template Tag	Description
<start no landmark>	First element in the Text Plan. No landmark near the area.
<start with landmark>	First element in the Text Plan. There is landmark near the area.
<body no landmark>	Elements between the first and the last element. No landmark near the area.
<body with landmark>	Elements between the first and the last element. There is landmark near the area.
<end no landmark>	Last element in the Text Plan. No landmark near the area.
<end with landmark>	First element in the Text Plan. There is landmark near the area.

Table 3. List of Template Tag

Once all the elements are analyzed, it will pass the Text Plan and the assigned templates to the next sub-module. Using the Text Plan in the previous module it will output the following:

<start no landmark><body no landmark> <body no landmark> <end no landmark>

Linguistic Realization

The template tags from the output of the discourse planning are the basis on what template number will be retrieved from the database. The database used in this sub-module contains all the templates with their corresponding tag. For every template randomly chosen, the values from the Text Plan are used to complete the template. Using the Text plan and the template tags it will output the following text:

- Simula sa De La Salle University, dumiretso pagkatapos kumanan sa Dagonoy.
  Translation: 'Starting from De La Salle University, you walk straight ahead and then turn right to Dagonoy'
- Pagkatapos lumiko, dumiretso lamang at kumaliwa sa Leon Guinto.
  Translation: 'After you turn, you walk straight and then turn left to Leon Guinto.'
- Ang susunod na gagawin ay hanapin ang Quirino at kumaliwa dito.
  Translation: 'The next step is to look for Quirino and turn left.'
- Dumiretso lamang at matatagpuan ang Ospital ng Maynila.
  Translation: 'You walk straight ahead and you will see the Hospital on Manila.'

Once the text form is generated it will then pass it to the SMS Processing Module to send back the message containing the route to the sender.

4 Evaluation

The quality of the routes generated was evaluated based on standards discussed by Lovelace, et al. (1999). According to Lovelace, et al. (1999), the quality of a route direction can be measured by the information present in the text. Examples of this information are the landmarks, turns and descriptive route information. To confirm the quality of the routed generated by our system two experiments were conducted.

Experiment 1: Unfamiliar route and Map

The goal of the experiment is to determine if a SMS response generated from the system is clear enough to direct a user to a safe place.

The task performed was to ask evaluators to answer a survey which contains an unfamiliar map and a route generated by the system. Following the route found in the survey, the evaluators need to draw lines on the roads of the map starting from a specified starting location going to the destination.

The survey was answered by 30 respondents, 14 of which are male while the rest are female. Below is a summary of the evaluation:

- Errors made by some respondents were through following the route per sentence. They go through the whole street that was mentioned in the first instruction before they head to the next street indicated in the next instruction. This result to mistakes in turning and the respondents had to go back since they missed a corner.
- Errors were caused due to unfamiliarity of the area, based from their drawing there are some lines that went over the corners and passed through them. These errors were due to the problem with the generation of the route. Roads that are going to a curve are sometimes perceived as a turn in direction.

Based from the results of this survey, some roads are hard to simulate by only looking at the map and the given route. It is recommended that an actual simulation is needed to test the reliability of the generated instruction.

Experiment 2: Validate Generated Route

The second experiment conducted is to evaluate the route generated whether it is effective in giving out directions.

Same as the previous experiment we ask evaluators to answer a survey. The survey was answered by 30 respondents, 14 of which are male while the rest are female. The survey contains an example route to be evaluated and a list of criteria made by Lovelace, et al. (1999). Evaluators were asked to check a criteria if it is present in the route generated by the system. Table 4 shows the result of the experiment.

Criteria	Votes	% *
A - Prepares the traveler for upcoming turning points to change location	21	70%
B - Mentions landmarks at turning points	21	70%
C - Gives 'you've gone too far if' statements in case a turning point is missed	18	60%
D - Gives landmarks rather than street names	14	47%
E - Provides a limited amount of redundant information	14	47%
F - Tells the traveler which way to proceed at a turning point to change location	23	77%
G - Provides information to allow recovery from errors	10	33%
H - Provides clearly linear information	20	67%
I - Gives distances between turning points	6	20%

* *no. of votes / no. of evaluators*

Table 4. Results of Experiment 2

The results show that the generated route was able to direct a user when there is a turning point to change direction. It is also observed that the route was able to use landmarks, but this is dependent on the data stored in the database. Criteria G and I are expected to be low because the templates used for the routes does not cover giving directions to allow recovery of errors and does not give distances between turning points.

5 Conclusion

The BahaBa System was able receive a SMS request, process the request, generate a route and its corresponding route message, and send the SMS back to the user.

Currently, the routes generated by the system are in the Filipino Language. But since we are using template-based NLG, it can easily be adapted to other languages by simply translating the templates that are stored in the database.

While experiment 1 results shows confusion among evaluators when navigating on the paper map, experiment 2 showed that the generated routes are effective. Possible future work includes, doing experiment 1 again but instead of navigating on paper map, an actual navigation should be done. Another possible work is on resolving the criteria G and I by reviewing and expanding the templates and adding more information relevant to route generation.

References

Dale, R., Geldof, S., & Prost, J.-P. (2003). CORAL: Using Natural Language Generation for Navigational Assistance. *26th Australasian Computer Science Conference - Volume 16* (pp. 35-44). Australian Computer Society, Inc.

Department of Science and Technology. (2013). *Project NOAH*. Retrieved January 2013, from Google Play: https://play.google.com/store/apps/details?id=ph.gov.dost.noah.android

Fajardo, J., & Oppus, C. (2012). A mobile disaster management system using the android technology. *WSEAS Transaction on Communications*, 9(6), 343-353.

Lovelace, K. L., Hegarty, M., & Montello, D. R. (1999). Elements of good route directions in familiar and unfamiliar environments. Spatial information theory. *Cognitive and computational foundations of geographic information science* (pp. 65-82). Berlin: Springer.

Nueva Caceres Technology Solutions, Inc. (2013). *iTyphoon*. Retrieved January 2013, from Google Play: https://play.google.com/store/apps/details?id=com.magnoconag.ITyphoon

The World Bank. (2012). *2012 Information and Communications and Development : Maximizing Mobile*. Washington DC: International Bank for Reconstruction and Development / The World Bank.

United Nations Economic and Social Commission for Asia and the Pacific and United Nations Office for Disaster Risk Reduction. (2012*). Asia Pacific Disaster Report 2012*. Bangkok, Thailand: United Nations Economic and Social Commission for Asia and the Pacific and United Nations International Strategy for Disaster Reduction.

United Nations Office for Disaster Risk Reduction. (2012). *Floods deaths down but economic losses significant*. Retrieved January 2013, from United Nations Office for Disaster Risk Reduction: http://www.unisdr.org/archive/30026

Author Index